Right Leadership

...Making Impact Today

Copyright © 2013 James Fadel

ISBN: 978-0-9895728-9-7

Published by:

Fadel Publishing International
515 Country Road 1118
Greenville, TX 75401

Printed in the United States of America

Dedication

To my wife,

Pastor (Mrs.) Dr. Manita Fadel.

You have been my love, my friend and my wife

for 24 years. Thank You!

Acknowledgments

There is a saying in Africa that it takes a family to give birth to a child but it takes a village to raise the child. This book would not have been possible without the support of many people.

I am grateful to my wife Pastor (Mrs.) Dr. Manita Fadel. She is the apple in my pie, the smile to my face, my love, who stood by me for 25 years. Thank you for giving me the time to work on this book. I equally appreciate your patience, encouragement and prayers.

I want to appreciate my three wonderful princesses: Tolani, Dara & Simi; I want to thank you for your support and understanding for the time I spent in writing this book. You are Scripts that have been written and yet to be read, you are Orchestras already composed and yet to be heard; you are my vision of what leaders will look like for the next generation. I am convinced that you will be signs and wonders to your own generation. I truly and deeply thank you.

Finally, very many thanks to my spiritual children and friends whom God used in one way or another to ensure that the dream to write this book became a reality: Pastor (Dr.) Sayo Ajiboye, Pastor Emmanuel O. Olaniran, Pastor Sola

Oloidi and Sister Lami Adama. They all ensured that the vision was kept alive. The Lord will reward you in Jesus name!

You are blessed in Jesus name!

Pastor James O. Fadel, DMin
Dallas, Texas
July 2013

TABLE OF CONTENTS

≈

Foreword

The body of literature on leadership has continued to blossom. And rightly so. Leadership, especially spiritual leadership, can not be over flogged. A proverb says a herd of Sheep led by a Lion will defeat a pride of Lions led by a Sheep.

No group can rise above its leader and there is a massive near-universal failure of good leadership in most areas or human endeavor. Potentials are never realized, destinies are truncated and opportunities are wasted as a direct result of failure of leadership.

"Right Leadership – Making Impact Today" by my spiritual son, James Fadel, is a welcome and an important contribution to the crucial task of identifying, nurturing and training spiritual leaders for the next generation.

He has laid out in easy-to-understand prose, the essentials of good spiritual leadership and the importance of moral uprightness. Personal discipline, robust preparation, patience and humility are all prerequisites carefully laid out by the author.

And of course, the foot prints, teaching and doctrine of Jesus Christ, is all over the book and is the foundation of the discourse.

Read, enjoy and become a spiritual leader as you reflect, meditate and apply the principles set forth in this work.

God bless you.

Pastor E.A. Adeboye
July 2013

Chapter One

What is Spiritual Leadership?

∽

Henry and Richard Blackaby clearly defined Spiritual Leadership as "moving people on to God's agenda" The implications in this definition are as follows:

1. The spiritual leader must move people from where they are to where God wants them to be. His or her duty is to inspire and guide them; his or her role is to lead them to that pathway where the only option that they have is the option that God has planned for them. Once the spiritual leader understands God's will, he or she makes every effort to move his or her followers from pursuing ordinary human agenda to pursuing God's purposes. Any leader who fails in the responsibility of mobilizing people to follow God's agenda has failed in leadership. Such a leader may have exhorted, cajoled, pleaded, or bullied the people; but they have not led the people until the people have chosen to adjust their lives to God's will.

2. Every spiritual leader must depend on the Holy Spirit: Spiritual leaders work within a context that is

paradoxical. This is because God has called them to accomplish goals that can be accomplished by God alone. The goals of a true spiritual leader cannot be accomplished by an ordinary man. Only the Holy Spirit can produce true spiritual transformation in people. Yet, the Spirit often chooses ordinary people and uses them to bring about spiritual growth in others. A good example is Moses in Exodus 3:7-8, 10:

Then the Lord told him, "I have certainly seen the oppression of my people in Egypt. I have heard their cries of distress because of their harsh slave drivers. Yes, I am aware of their suffering. ⁸ So I have come down to rescue them from the power of the Egyptians and lead them out of Egypt into their own fertile and spacious land. It is a land flowing with milk and honey – the land where the Canaanites, Hittites, Amorites, Perizzites, Hivites, and Jebusites now live. ¹⁰ Now go, for I am sending you to Pharaoh. You must lead my people Israel out of Egypt."

Spiritual Leaders are accountable to God: Leaders do not blame their followers when they don't do what they should do, just as a teacher has not taught until students have learned. Godly leaders have acute responsibilities and should not make excuses because their responsibility primarily is to move people to do the will of God

Spiritual leaders can influence all people, not just God's people: God's agenda applies to the marketplace as well as the meeting place. Although, spiritual leaders will generally induce God's people to achieve God's purposes, God can use them to exert significant godly influence upon unbelievers. An example is Joseph – God's plan was to spare the Egyptians from a devastating seven-year famine so that through the Egyptians, Middle Eastern people will be adequately provided for. History is replete with examples of Christian men and women exerting spiritual leadership upon secular society.

3. Spiritual leaders work from God's agenda: The greatest obstacle to effective spiritual leadership is people pursuing their own agendas rather than seeking God's will.

Too often, unseasoned leaders assume that the role of a leader is solely in the responsibility of determining what should be done. They therefore assume aggressive personae, develop aggressive goals; they dream grandiose dreams and cast grand visions. After choosing such agendas, they begin to pray and ask the Lord to join them in their agenda and bless their efforts. How disappointing! That is not what true spiritual leaders do. True spiritual leaders seek God's will, they marshal their people to pur- sue God's plan.

Chapter Two

The Prerequisites of a Leader

~

Aprerequisite is that thing which we require so that we can achieve our goal or carry out our mission. For instance, a prerequisite course of study must be completed before enrolling in another course.

In order to be truly successful, we must first have a clear grasp of the prerequisite. Such a clear grasp also guarantees efficient relationships, which assures the continuity of victory by the spiritual leader. Everyone gravitates toward success and to achieve the status of success in leadership; we must be equipped with certain fundamental principles; these principles are essential for success

Now that we understand Spiritual leadership, what are the prerequisites to be a spiritual leader? When God searches the earth for potential leaders, what does he look for? It is certain that he does not look out for men who are angels or people who are perfect since there is none. Rather, he searches for ordinary men and women with certain outstanding qualities. In 1 Samuel 13:13-14, God was searching for a man whose heart is similar to the heart and the mind of the divine trinity. He chose David and called him a man "after my own heart".

> *"How foolish!" Samuel exclaimed. "You have not kept the command the Lord your God gave you. Had you kept it, the Lord would have established your kingdom over Israel forever. [14]But now your kingdom must end, for the Lord has sought out a man after his own heart. The Lord has already appointed him to be the leader of his people, because you have not kept the Lord's command."*

David did not look different from any other Jewish boys of his age. He was simply of distinctive physical appearance. The Bible makes it clear in 1 Samuel 16:12 thus:

> *So he sent and brought him in and he was ruddy, with bright eyes, and good-looking. And the LORD said, "Arise, anoint him; for this is the one!"*

To illustrate this point further, read below the way that the New American Standard Bible describes the situation:

> *He was ruddy, with beautiful eyes and a handsome appearance.*

In this place, Samuel was describing what he saw like any other human being with the gift of sight. Samuel was not an angel. This is why the Bible states:

> *"For the eyes of the LORD run to and fro throughout the whole earth, to show Himself strong on behalf of those whose heart is loyal to Him."*

Looking through the scriptures, we will discover that out of all the Biblical characters, David has the most chapters dedicated to his life story. Fourteen chapters are dedicated to Abraham, eleven chapters talked about Joseph and Jacob, while ten chapters are dedicated to Elijah. Sixty six chapters talked about David, and these do not include fifty nine references to his life in the New Testament. God chooses the nobodies and turns them into somebodies.

The Greeks of the bible age are like most people today. They focused solely on surface issues as their basis for judging others, and they make decisions based on what is apparent. For example, to determine how beautiful or brilliant or successful a person is, the Greeks will look at a myriad of surface issues. This generation is like the Greeks in this regard, the superficial impress us. When we watch television for instance, how people look on television is more important to this generation than how they truly are in real life. God is not impressed by "stuff!" He is a God that is of substance, he is looking for extremely specific characteristics. God is an eternal designer; all his products are made to fit.

God always call men who are not qualified and prepare them for the assigned tasks/assignments. This is revealed in 1 Corinthians 1:26-29:

> *Remember, dear brothers and sisters, that few of you were wise in the world's eyes or powerful or wealthy when God called you. [27] Instead, God chose things the world considers foolish in order to shame those who think they are wise. And he chose things that are powerless to shame those who*

9

are powerful. [28] *God chose things despised by the world; things counted as nothing at all, and used them to bring to nothing what the world considers important.* [29] *As a result, no one can ever boast in the presence of God.*

The Lord gives both death and life; he brings some down to the grave but raises others up. The Lord makes some poor and others rich; he brings some down and lifts others up. [8] *He lifts the poor from the dust and the needy from the garbage dump He sets them among princes, placing them in seats of honor. For all the earth is the Lord's, and he has set the world in order.*

(1 Samuel 2:6-8b)

Total Dependency on God:

In John 5:19, Jesus said: *I tell you the truth, the Son can do nothing by himself.* Remember He is the Son of God, the Word became flesh, and the express image of the Father, yet He said He could do nothing without God.

Again, in John 5:30, He said *I can do nothing on my own initiative* meaning He didn't initiate a single thing. He was totally dependent upon His Father.

He goes on to state in John 5:19: *So Jesus explained, "I tell you the truth, the Son can do nothing by himself. He does only what he sees the Father doing. Whatever the Father does, the Son also does."*

His instruction to us is, *without Me you can do nothing* (John 15:5b). God requires total and absolute dependency on God. He is a specialist in using weak people! He singles out a person, he prepares him, and he imparts His Spirit on him so that he can fulfill His plan. **In Psalm 44:1-3** the Bible states:

> *O God, we have heard it with our own ears – our ances- tors have told us of all you did in their day, in day's long ago² You drove out the pagan nations by your power and gave all the land to our ancestors. You crushed their enemies and set our ancestors free. ³ They did not conquer the land with their swords; it was not their own strong arm that gave them victory. It was your right hand and strong arm and the blinding light from your face that helped them, for you loved them.*

Spirituality:

The Lord sought out David as a man after His own heart (1 Samuel 13:14). David was a man whose life was in harmony with God and he was focused on what was necessary to God. He was a vessel who adhered strictly to the commands of God. He was sensitive to the things of God, and he submitted to divine dealings so that his life could conform to the purpose of God for his life. God is searching for a heart that is completely His.

> *"The eyes of the Lord search the whole earth in order to strengthen those whose hearts are fully committed to him. What a fool you have been! Now you will be at war."*

> **(2 Chronicles 16:9)**

To such people, there are no locked closets; nothing is swept under the rug. They are only involved in matters that satisfy the Master while they long and strive to please Him in their thoughts and actions. They care about the motivations behind their actions because their

11

main concern is to glorify God. And this is depicted in **1 Samuel 2:3:**

> *"Stop acting so proud and haughty! Don't speak with such arrogance! For the Lord is a God who knows what you have done; he will judge your actions."*

(1 Samuel 2:3)

Chapter Three

A Generation is Passing

⌒

A merican banking community faces a critical challenge right now. By the end of 2012, one out of every five CEOs has taken a voluntary retirement. The question that arose in many boardrooms is this: Who will take their place?[1] It is not just in the world of banking that this reality rules. The same challenge faces many industries. Listed below are a list of Professions and the percentage of workers who are above 55 years old in 2013.[2]

2012 Occupations with Oldest Jobholders				
Occupation	No. Jobs	Ages of Jobholders (%)		
	(000s)	55-64	65+	55+
Funeral service managers	13	23.1%	38.5%	61.5%
Motor vehicle operators, all other	63	15.9%	39.7%	55.6%
Legislators	11	27.3%	27.3%	54.5%
Model makers and patternmakers, metal and plastic	11	45.5%	9.1%	54.5%
Farmers, ranchers, and other agricultural managers	944	26.4%	26.7%	53.1%
Judges, magistrates, and other judicial workers	67	38.8%	11.9%	50.7%
Proofreaders and copy markers	10	40.0%	10.0%	50.0%

[1] Reed, Candice. 2012 Post-boomers wait not so patiently in the wings. *The Free Library* (October,10),http://www.thefreelibrary.com/Post-boomers_wait not so patiently in the wings.-a0306358950 (accessed July 20 2013)

[2] http://money.usnews.com/money/blogs/the-best-life/2013/06/19/challenges-of-an-aging-american-workforce

Occupation	No. Jobs (000s)	Ages of Jobholders (%)		
		55-64	65+	55+
Print binding and finishing workers	22	36.4%	13.6%	50.0%
Tool and die makers	56	39.3%	8.9%	48.2%
Postal service clerks	148	43.9%	3.4%	47.3%
Clergy	408	29.4%	17.2%	46.6%
Crossing guards	61	23.0%	23.0%	45.9%
Bus drivers	558	29.9%	15.6%	45.5%
Travel agents	73	21.9%	21.9%	43.8%
Embalmers and funeral attendants	16	6.3%	37.5%	43.8%
Sociologists	7	28.6%	14.3%	42.9%
Religious workers, all other	69	24.6%	17.4%	42.0%
Models, demonstrators, and product promoters	65	27.7%	13.8%	41.5%
Construction and building inspectors	118	33.9%	7.6%	41.5%
Judicial law clerks	17	35.3%	5.9%	41.2%
Source: U.S. Bureau of Labor Statistics				

According to the US Census Bureau, 10,000 people will turn 65 every day until 2030. This oft-cited statistic is already impacting conversations around health care, caregiving and the economy.

The Church and an Aging Workforce: It is important to note that leadership of the Church of Christ is in this endangered leadership zone. According to this data, a solid 54% of all Church workers in the United States are Seniors!

In Europe, the Roman Catholic Church is so impacted by this dearth of leaders that it now must import priests from Africa and Asia. According to New York Times of April 7th 2013, the Church in France must now be sustained by
"a battalion of priests who have come to France from abroad —

14

from places like Benin, Burkina-Faso, Cameroon but also Viet-nam and Poland" [3] *"In France… Magnificent churches dot the country, but France's clergy is old and ordinations of priests are in continuing decline. The average age of France's 14,000 priests is 72."*

Even though we may not have an efficiently focused data on the Pentecostal arm of the American Church, they may not fare much better than the Roman Catholics. In a 2001 research, Hartford Institute for Religion Research has this to say (and it is on their website):

"In the past few decades, men and women have been entering the ministry at older ages. Most had another career before going to seminary, and by the time they settled into the role of minister they tended to be middle-aged. **In a recent study, the median age of senior or solo Protestant pastors was 51. The median age of senior or solo black pastors was 53.** *Roman Catholic priests are the oldest; their median age was 56.*
Associate pastors and those serving in non-church settings tended to be slightly younger. In a 2001 report by the U.S. Bureau of Labor Statistics the median age of full-time, graduate-educated minister was 45." [4]

It is very instructive to further note the data from Pew Forum on the Age of members of Evangelical Churches. [5] A full 83% of attendance is above 30 years!

---

[3] http://www.nytimes.com/2013/04/08/world/europe/foreign-clergy-move-to-france-to-aid-catholics.html?pagewanted=all&_r=0
[4] http://hirr.hartsem.edu/research/fastfacts/fast_facts.html#pastage
[5] http://religions.pewforum.org/portraits

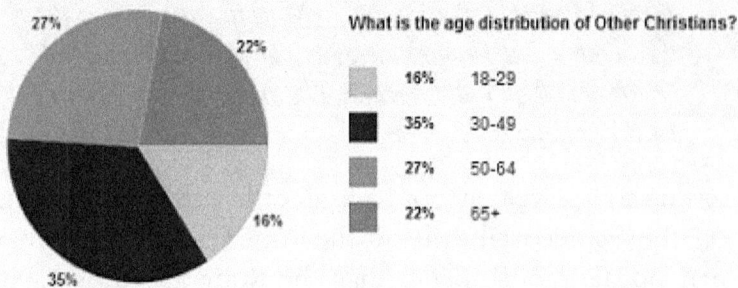

What is the age distribution of Other Christians?

	16%	18-29
	35%	30-49
	27%	50-64
	22%	65+

If we compare the Church Demographics with the population distribution of the United States of America in the 2010 US Census; it becomes clear that there is an inverse relationship: the Church is essentially standing on its head!

A US Census Bureau projection shows this trend between 1909 and 2015. This is Year 2013; we stand right at the edge of this major National Projection; it says one thing and one thing alone: No leader worth his salt can ignore the Next Generation.

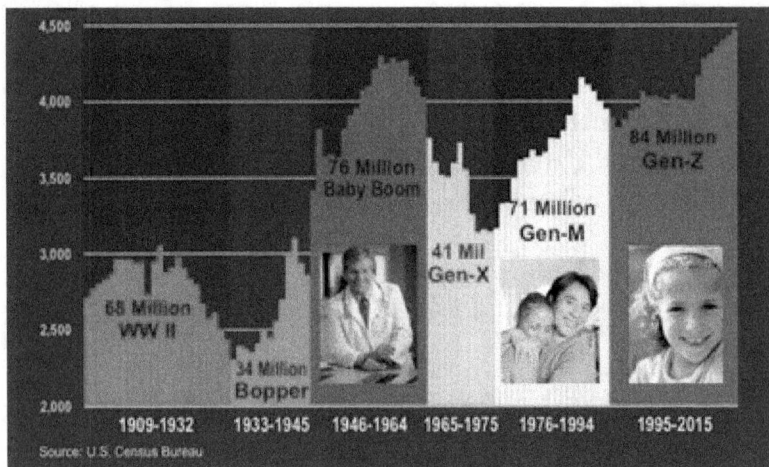

Tightening the Gospel Buckle of the Bible Belt: The 2010 National Census showed that the State of Texas has a population of 25,145,561 individuals. This population has since grown tremendously over the past three years! Out of this number, a full 11,245,529 are below 30 years of age. That is a full 44.72 % of the population. If the Church of Christ has access to only 17% of this total, the implication is that we are in a deficit of 9,333, 789 individuals who are below the age of 30 years. We are excluded from impacting these lives! If this is so in Texas, which is the core and the Buckle of the American Bible Belt; what then is the situation in the Rust Belt Regions and the Western expanses of the nation who are traditionally more resistant to the Church and the Gospel? The American Church has a lively challenge on her hand!

TX - Texas	
Age / Sex	
Total Population : 25,145,561	
Male	12,472,280
Female	12,673,281
Under 18	6,865,824
18 and over	18,279,737
20-24	1,817,079
25-34	3,613,473
35-49	5,218,849
50 -64	4,272,560
65 & over	2,601,886
Zoom In I Compare I Print	

Chapter Four

Understanding Generations

☞

One of the wise sayings of the ancient people of China goes thus:

"One generation opens the road upon which another generation travels."

The Holy Scriptures also have this to say:

[3] Great is the LORD, and greatly to be praised; and his greatness is unsearchable.
[4] One generation shall praise your works to another, and shall declare your mighty acts.
[5] I will speak of the glorious honor of your majesty, and of your wondrous works.

(Psalm 145:3-5)

Since 1662 when John Gaunt produced the first major study in modern Cohorts and found out that two thirds of children born in London in that era died before their 16th birthday, it has become useful to seek an understanding of Generational Cohorts[1].

---

1 Gaunt, John (1662), *Natural and Political Observations Made upon the Bills of Mortality*

A Generational Cohort is defined as follows:

> *"the group of individuals (within some population definition) who experience the same event within the same time interval"*[2]

In a study going back to the 15th century, William Strauss and Neil Howie in their book, *"Generations and the Fourth Turning;"* described an engaging perspective on history with a focus on the American continent. They viewed history from a cyclical perspective that is fully dependent and connected to the cycle of a long human life *(between 80 and 100 years).*

The Romans called this cycle a *saeculum* or *siècle* and it is translated in modern English as the word *century.* Strauss and Howie broke this down further into what they called the half stroke of the human life cycle or the Kondratieff wave *(40 to 50 years)* and finally into the four phases of human experience each about 20 years in length. The Greeks called each of these four phases a *genos* and we call them *generations.* Strauss and Howie showed how this force has been respected across eons and in every civilization. They quoted Judges 2:10 which talked about *"another generation… who did not know the Lord nor what he had done for Israel."* According to them, history get its underlying beat from *saeculum,* it gets its seasonal variety from *genos. Genos has four archetypes;* they define the direction of nations and peoples.

---

[2] Klauke, Amy. (2000) Coping with Changing Demographics. Webpage at ERICDigests.org. An analysis of the effect of changing demographic patterns on school enrollments and education.

A genos is formed by shared experiences. Each of us has personal markers of life and time. There are key events and occurrences that are unforgettable and that impacted us. Each of us is either being shaped by what Strauss and Howie referred to as our *early markers,* or we are shaping lives through the *late markers* that we create and help facilitate. It is the linkage of biological aging and shared experiences that make history relevant.

Strauss and Howie define a generation as the aggregate of people born over the span of a phase of life who share a common location in history and understand that in time, they all must perish. A generation feels *"the same historical urgency,"* around the same time; and they have a collective communal psyche. A generation is a product of history and by its very existence; a maker of history. There is a symbiotic linkage between history, time and a cohort.

Previous generations have often failed widely in predicting their successors. This failure has often been due to an assumption that succeeding generations will adopt the values of the old. What has happened instead has been a stubborn commitment to the redefinition of self, time and space. Strauss and Howie analyzed different generations from 1883 to the late 2000s and used the following adjectives to define them.

Generational Identity	Year in which Generation was Born	Characteristic Adjectives
The Lost Generation	1883 - 1900	Cautionary Individualists
The GI Generation	1901 - 1924	Hubristic, launched America into an expansive era of affluence, global power and civic planning. Ethics of this Generation was defined by Confidence
The Silent Generation	1925 – 1942	Experts, Sensitive operators, conformists. They fine-tuned the GI Generations hubris, sustained the Institutional order created while simultaneously managing the passion of youth. Ethics of this Generation was Conciliatory and the Social Order was Individuated.
Boomer Generation	1943 – 1960	Narcissistic, asserted the primacy of self, confronted social and institutional order and perceived it as vacuous. Ethics of the Boomers were Confrontational and Judgmental
13th Generation or Generation X	1961 - 1981	Neglected, unprotected, severely exposed at a time of massive cultural convulsion and adult self-discovery. It is the first generation to experience the widespread impact of divorce, single parent childhood and are often referred to as the "latchkey kids." It is the 13th Generation to call itself American. Ethics of this Generation is pragmatic and there is a focus on Survivalism that was born out of necessity. This is a skeptical generation whose first question is often "what is in it for me." It is probably the most highly educated generation in American history. 29% of this generation has a college degree.
Millennial or Gen Y	1977 - 1995	Treasured, protected and provided for *(Soccer Mom Phenomenon!)*. Highly sophisticated, technologically and financially savvy, immune to most traditional marketing pitch. A racially and ethnically diverse generation.
Generation Z	1995 - 2012	Highly diverse environment, highly sophisticated media culture, still evolving!

Generational Archetypes: Straus and Howie defined 4 generational archetypes. Each archetype responds to the context of the environment when they were born.

i.   *A Prophets Generation* is born during *a High*

ii. *A Nomad Generation* is born during an *Awakening*

iii. *A Hero Generation* is born during an *Unravelling*

iv. *An Artist Generation* is born during a *Crisis*

The GI Generations were Heroes and the Silent Generations were Artists. The Boomer Generations were largely Prophets and the Gen X-ers were Nomads. The Saecular cycle is turning right around to produce Millennials who are tending towards becoming Heroes!

It is that season in times when leaders must consciously make a way and create the road upon which a new generation must travel.

Chapter Five

Voices from the Past

Philosophy, Philosophers & Generational Engagement

❦

Voices from the past can contribute to understanding the evolution of the present. A quick survey of ancient philosophers will assist us in understanding the strategic mandate of reaching the Next Generations and effectively working with them.

Pilate and Truth

He was the Fifth Prefect that Rome sent to the Province of Judaea. He was granted the opportunity to be the judge at the greatest trial ever and he sat in judgment over the creator of the Universe. He tossed the judgment in favor of the fear of man and he failed to provide the leadership required at a critical junction in history. He was not aware that the judgment, which he delivered, was a judgment on his own eternal future: his name was Pontius Pilate. Pontius voice rings across many generations because he raised the core question that every leader and every philosopher must ask. Pilate summarized the question in every leader's heart; he asked Jesus: "what is truth."[1]

---

[1] John 18:38

25

What is truth is a heart question. It is a leadership question that must ring in every clime. The answer to this question has shaped and will shape many generations for good or for bad. For Pilate, this question became a source of pain, infamy and eventual destruction. For many leaders across generations, their answer when confronted with the question has made a Pilate out of them. The leadership of the Next Generation must learn that Truth is a rock of offence. It is the rock at which we must not fall.

Socrates and Generation Next: Concerning the Logos and the Pursuit of the Inner Sight:

Socrates came to truth from a negative platform. He is it that is reputed to have famously said, *"I know that I know nothing."* Because of this perspective, Socrates developed the Elenctic system of education. In it, he asks negative question after negative question believing that after a rigorous process of weeding out what is not, we will find out what is. Socrates was searching for *the logos*. His goal was to rigorously examine every proposition till he found out the *logos*. It is instructive to note that John the Beloved started out his writings in the Gospel with the statement

"En archē ēn ho Lógos.., In the beginning, the logos."[2]

Socrates focuses on the power of the *Muses* to impact man's insight into matter. Greek Muses are personifications of knowledge and inspiration, they control internally directed actions. Socrates insists that the Muses influence knowing and makes what is knowable to far exceed what is real by a great length. According to Socrates, that which is truthfully real lies in the realm of that which cannot be

---

2   John 1:1

26

grasped by the physical hands of man. Socrates believed strongly that living without divine inspiration restricts the access of the leader to true and higher insight.

Finally, Socrates believed that the leader who receives insight from the Muses must come to the marketplace of life and ideas and implement the insight that he or she received. He or she must be required, nay, forced; to make his or her insight accessible among ordinary humans who may not have similar gifts of inner sight.

We interpret Socrates as theorizing that Insight *(inner sight)* is a gift from the divine. It is a gift that must be shared. Socrates is convinced that the highest wisdom that the masses can muster is totally dependent on the access of the Philosopher King into the insight that the Muses grant.

Generation Next is characterized by a desire to focus on that which is internal and personal rather than on that which is external and lifeless. In this, Socrates who was accused of corrupting the youths of Athens seems to speak from across the eons to a new generation of young people. He seems to encourage the pursuit of inner sight.

Christian doctrine describes this inner sight as the illumination of the Holy Spirit. The great Prophet Isaiah describes it thus in **Isaiah 30:20-21**:

> [20] *And though the Lord give you the bread of adversity, and the water of affliction, yet shall not your teachers be removed into a corner any more, but your eyes shall see your teachers:* [21] *And your ears shall hear a word behind you, saying, This is the way, walk you in it, when you turn to the right hand, and when you turn to the left.*

The great Apostle John describes it thus in **John 16:13**

> *[13] However, when he, the Spirit of truth, is come, he will guide you into all truth: for he shall not speak of himself; but whatever he shall hear, that shall he speak: and he will show you things to come.*

Generation Next is perfectly right in its desire to demand the reinterpretation of form around that which is insubstantial. There is a need – however, to understand that the insubstantiality is not unreality. The insubstantiality is rooted in the lecture of our Lord with Nicodemus in **John 3:8**

> *The wind blows where it wants, and you hear the sound thereof, but can not tell from where it comes, and where it goes: so is every one that is born of the Spirit.*

The leadership of Generation Next must act in the Spirit and by the Spirit.

Plato and Generation Next: Concerning the Rule of Wisdom and the Philosopher King:

Plato practically laid the foundation of Western Philosophy. A student of Socrates, Plato founded one of the earliest formal schools known to Western Civilization. One of his core focuses is to understand the structure of the society as a caste creating system that streams men into roles as workers, warriors or philosopher kings. Plato is famously noted to have said *"cities and human race will have no rest from evil until philosopher kings adequately philosophize."*[3]

---

[3] *Republic* 473c-d

Plato's philosopher king must "love the sight of truth" [4] and all of education must be tailored to produce these philosopher kings who will rule the ideal city. Plato's ideal city slightly differs from Socrates. While Socrates saw a city of farmers, craftsmen, merchants, and practicing workmen, Plato's city was a city of luxury with a number of other occupations that the presence of the philosopher king introduces and necessitates. Thus Plato believes that the highest form of leadership is aristocracy, which he described as the rule by the best. The lowest form is tyranny, which he described as the rule by one. Plato distinguishes between tyranny and aristocracy by insisting that aristocracy is the rule by the philosopher king whose focus is on wisdom and reason. These two characteristics are supplied by the inner sight, which Socrates taught. Tyranny on the other hand arises from the breakdown of democracy *(the second lowest form of ruler-ship)* and the rise of an undisciplined society. The normative characteristic of such a society is violence. The society is controlled by a "champion" who controls a private army and oppresses those who are not in his employ.

Plato, who wrote extensively; also displayed a deep distrust for the written word. He insisted that the best method of passing critically important information is **one-on-one** through trusted channels. In this he alludes to a mentoring process that was evidently the means with which he was trained. Plato, like his teacher Socrates; defaults to the Logos. He seems to validate Apostle Paul's injunction in 2 Timothy 2:2:

> *And the things which thou hast heard from me among many witnesses, the same* **commit** *thou to* **faithful men**, *who shall be able to teach others also.*

---

[4] *Republic* 475

When Plato gave what was considered as his most important discuss, it was verbal and not written. His focus was interestingly on *The One.* He referred to this One as Unity, the causal factor for Good and the differentiator of the dyadic twin of Good - Evil. [5]

Not A Rule By An Undifferentiated Masses: Though not a perfect treatise, Plato's position screams of excellence. One could almost cry out loud that Generation Next will not settle for the rule of an undifferentiated mass. One is stirred to pray that Generation Next will accept the challenge of developing their inner sight so that they will be empowered to become Philosopher-Kings. One is stirred to pray that Generation Next will somehow access what was obvious to Plato who lived before Christ. That democracy as good as it looks may require an upgrading. That as the Philosopher – Kings arise among Generation-Next, they will somehow reject the temptation to amass private armies and abuse power in the mode of archetypal Tyrants.

Aristotle and Generation Next – Concerning Being and Potentiality:

Maybe no one affected every facet of study in the West as much as Aristotle. There is no philosopher that also impacted Jews, Christians and Muslims like him. For the purposes of our study, we will focus on Aristotelian presentation on Being and Potentiality. Apart from the Supreme Cause whom Aristotle called the *unmovable mover who orders the pathways of the planetary and terrestrial beings – primum movens immobile;* every being on earth – humans es-

---

[5] Aristotle. *Aristotle's Metaphysics,* ed. W.D. Ross. Oxford: Clarendon Press. 1924. (See http://www.perseus.tufts.edu/hopper/text?doc=Perseus:text:1999.01. 0051:book=1:section=980a&redirect=true)

pecially have a *Being* which is an ideal estate of existence that represents the *Actuality* of the person. The estate of *being* is perfect, it is full; it is a realization of all that is; it encompasses the totality of all that will be.

Aristotle posits that for *Beings* to *Be,* that is for us to truly claim to *be;* there must be a higher and a purer actuality, a primordial matter that attracts all things to himself. Heaven for instance emanated from this causal being because of a desire to be associated with His beauty. This immovable Being lays in an eternal self-contemplative thought and draws all things into himself and into a continuously productive or procreative motion - just by his eternal immovable beauty and repose. In this manner, an *eternal heaven, drawn into the presence of this eternal life; gives birth to an eternally productive time and an eternally sustainable world system.*

Aristotelian conviction is that in this Eternal Unmovable Being, all existence has an indestructible *actuality.* Aristotle essentially affirms the eternity of Man.

Pauline Allusion to Aristotle: In Acts 17 while speaking on Mars Hill to Athenian elite, Apostle Paul alluded to this core Aristotelian thought when he stated, *"your own poets have said, we are all his offspring!*

> [24] *"The God who made the world and everything in it is the Lord of heaven and earth and does not live in temples built by hands.*
> [25] *And he is not served by human hands, as if he needed anything, because he himself gives all men life and breath and everything else.*
> [26] *From one man he made every nation of men, that they should inhabit the whole earth; and he determined the times*

set for them and the exact places where they should live.
²⁷God did this so that men would seek him and perhaps reach out for him and find him, though he is not far from each one of us.
²⁸'For in him we live and move and have our being.' As some of your own poets have said, 'We are his offspring.'
²⁹"Therefore since we are God's offspring, we should not think that the divine being is like gold or silver or stone--an image made by man's design and skill.

Aristotle and Potentiality: Aristotle expanded on this connect between this Being and human experience by describing **Potentiality.** Potentiality describes our estate now. It describes the imperfection of being, his and her incompleteness; it describes the possibility of our perfectibility: it affirms that we all are a work in progress.

Being a Work In Progress: Generation Next must be at home with the fact of our being a work in progress. We know from Aristotle and more also from the Scriptures that as we draw closer to God who is *all actuality* (*Actus Purus* in Latin), we will be changed. He will *set us in motion* towards a Journey for Excellence and Perfection.

> *And we, who with unveiled faces all reflect the Lord's glory, are being transformed into his likeness with ever-increasing glory, which comes from the Lord, who is the Spirit.*

> **(2 Corinthians 3:18)**

Many in Generation Next are waiting for the day when they can be perfect before assuming the service call associated with leadership. The Scriptures and Aristotle teach that this is totally unnecessary. Generation Next must serve in faith, where they are and as they are. As this generation serves and leads confident that God who is *"All Actuality"* is their God, their **Potentiality** will be changed into **Actuality**.

> *But he said to me, "My grace is sufficient for you, for my power is made perfect in weakness." Therefore I will boast all the more gladly about my weaknesses, so that Christ's power may rest on me.*
>
> **(2 Corinthians 12:9)**

A Wisdom Tale About Rabbi Zusia

Once, the great Hassidic leader, Zusia, came to his followers. His eyes were red with tears, and his face was pale with fear.

"Zusia, what's the matter? You look frightened!"

"The other day, I had a vision. In it, I learned the question that the angels will one day ask me about my life."

The followers were puzzled. "Zusia, you are pious. You are scholarly and humble. You have helped so many of us. What question about your life could be so terrifying that you would be frightened to answer it?"

Zusia turned his gaze to heaven. "I have learned that the angels will not ask me, 'Why weren't you a Moses, leading your people out of slavery?'"

His followers persisted. "So, what will they ask you?"

"And I have learned," Zusia sighed, "that the angels will not ask me, 'Why weren't you a Joshua, leading your people into the promised land?'"

33

One of his followers approached Zusia and placed his hands on Zusia's shoulders. Looking him in the eyes, the follower demanded, "But what will they ask you?"

"They will say to me, 'Zusia, there was only one thing that no power of heaven or earth could have prevented you from becoming.' They will say, 'Zusia, why weren't you Zusia?"

The moral of this tale is simple, no one will ask this generation "why were you not like your fathers and mothers?" Succeeding generations will question each and every one of them, however; and the question will be simply: "Did you become yourself?"

Chapter Six

The Shepherd's Heart

❧

I believe the difference between a shepherd and a hireling is that a shepherd has genuine love and care for the sheep. A shepherd binds up the wounds of the sheep, and he or she pours in the oil of healing. If someone is not a shepherd, he or she simply does the job for a paycheck. Jesus Christ is our perfect example of a shepherd, it is imperative that we follow His example. We see a full description of this scenario from **John 10:11-14:**

> I am the good shepherd. The good shepherd sacrifices his life for the sheep. *12*A hired hand will run when he sees a wolf coming. He will abandon the sheep because they don't belong to him and he isn't their shepherd. And so the wolf attacks them and scatters the flock. *13*The hired hand runs away because he's working only for the money and doesn't really care about the sheep. *14*"I am the good shepherd; I know my own sheep, and they know me."

David loved the sheep in his care so much that he went out of his way to make them safe (1 Samuel 17:33-35). What an attitude. The prophets of old reprimand the shepherds because of their attitude toward the sheep.

They were insensitive towards the sheep and failed to bond with those who were broken or help those who were diseased. *Hirelings* use the flock to gratify and satisfy their own needs, but Jesus, the good shepherd; lays down His life for the sheep **(John 10:11).**

(A) *The Shepherd is Humble:* It seemed like the God of Heaven set up a surveillance camera in the home of Jesse and spotted David. As God watched the thoughts and the actions of this young man, he could do only one thing, which was to exclaim, "That's my man!"

> *"Find a man named Jesse who lives there, for I have selected one of his sons to be my king."*
>
> **(1 Samuel 16:1b)**

Edward Marbury asserts that, "A humble man has this advantage over a proud man, for he cannot fall." And Thomas Watson intones "A humble sinner is in a better condition than a proud angel." The Puritans used to say that, "Pride is the last thing that leaves the human heart, and the first thing that returns."

David was faithful in keeping his father's sheep while his brothers were pulling ranks in Saul's army (Psalm 78:70; 89:10). What a humble man! The word "humble" comes from the Latin word *humus*. It means earthy, like the dirt, down to earth. Down to earth people are free from a sense of superiority and *elitism*. Show me a person who has a good character, and I will show you a man who has God's image imprinted on his heart. Yes, he or she may not have certain temperament, or the right charisma, and or a proven track record. But as long as he is authentic, people feel drawn to him rather than repelled. Above all, in James 4:6, the Bible states that God resists the proud, but gives grace to the humble.

(B) ***The Shepherd is a Servant:*** A humble person has the heart of a servant, he chooses to do what he's told; he or she does not rebel. He or she respects those who are in charge and serves in a faithful and a quiet manner. As a servant, he or she has one great goal and that is to make the person he serves look better and to make that person even more successful than he is presently. Also, he does not want the person he serves to fail. In other words, he does not care who gets the glory, his main focus is to get the job done. While David's brothers were off in the army making rank their focus and fighting big, impressive battles, David was all alone in the wilderness keeping the sheep. He had nothing to play games with or something to project his self-worth on or a platform to prove himself from. He had nothing to *lose (doesn't have to guard his reputation or fear he'd lose popularity),* nothing to *hide (keep up the facade or image for anyone).* He was vulnerable and transparent. It is interesting to note that almost every person who made impact in their generation had a servant heart. Some of them are identified below.

- Elisha served Elijah.
- Gehazi served Elisha.
- Naaman was the servant of the king of Syria.
- The men who encouraged Naaman were his servants.
- The little maid was the servant of Naaman's wife.

> *This letter is from Paul, a slave of Christ Jesus, chosen*
> *by God to be an apostle and sent out to preach his Good*
> *News.*
>
> **(Romans 1:1)**

(C) ***A Shepherd has a Clear Identity:*** Paul knew what
he was called to be. Do you know what you are called
to be? In the Bible, a bondservant serves his master
faithfully for six years, in the seventh year, the law
requires that he or she be set fee. But if when he
was released, he returned to his Master and said, "I
am not serving you because I have to, I am serving
you because I want to", then the master could decide
to take him before a judge and pierce his ears,
signifying that he belonged to him forever.

> *But the slave may declare, 'I love my master, my wife,*
> *and my children. I don't want to go free.' ⁶If he does*
> *this, his master must present him before God. Then*
> *his master must take him to the door or doorpost and*
> *publicly pierce his ear with an awl. After that, the slave*
> *will serve his master for life.*
>
> **(Exodus 21:5-6)**

Sometimes we need to say the same thing to the Lord:

> *I'm not serving you because I deeply want to, I'm serving*
> *you because I love to. Pierce my ears Lord. Make me*
> *yours. Bond me together with You so I can never belong*
> *to another!*

(D) ***Shepherding is a Ministry (Ministry as a Noun):***
In the economy of heaven, ministry is a noun and
not a verb. Ministry flows from who we are and

it is not necessarily what we do. The Word that forms the foundation of every true ministry is alive, it has the ability to speak, it walks and commands others to walk; it demands multiple journeys across great distances: it does all of these activities with the passion of a living being. When ministry loses its passion, it becomes an empty profession. Ministry changes from being a **noun into simply being a verb. It becomes dead works!**

At a lower level of service, ministry identifies with *what someone* **claims** *to do*. Ministry is deeper than claims, it is what you are which prompts you to act, and to do to a level of absolute efficiency, to the point there is total identification of the person with the service. In Ministry, you are expected to be what you claim, you are supposed to identify – totally.

Paint this powerful picture from the times of the Romans. The word servant referred to a third level gallery slave chained to the oar of a Roman ship. Day and night, **he rowed to the beat of another,** and whether he was in battle for a nation or in a merchant's service, he is expected to die chained to the oar. What a picture!

This picture brings to mind the words of Apostle Paul in **Romans 12:1.**

And so, dear brothers and sisters, I plead with you to give your bodies to God because of all he has done for you. Let them be a living and holy sacrifice – the kind he will find acceptable. This is truly the way to worship him.

(E) *The Shepherd Has Integrity:* Integrity! God is not looking for magnificent specimens of humanity. He is looking for deeply spiritual and genuinely humble who are honest- to-the-core. For example, Psalms 78:71-72 states that:

> *He took David from tending the ewes and lambs and made him the shepherd of Jacob's descendants – God's own people, Israel. [72] He cared for them with a true heart and led them with skillful hands.*

Warren W. Wiersbe explains what integrity means in *The Integrity Crisis.* The Oxford English Dictionary states that the word comes from Latin *integritas,* which means "wholeness," "entireness," "completeness." The root word is *integer* which means "untouched," "intact," "entire." Integrity is to the personal or corporate character, what health is to the physical body or 20/20 vision is to the human eyes. A person with integrity is not divided because the division of a person's heart guarantees duplicity. A person with integrity does not merely pretend or put on a show because that will be hypocrisy. He or she is "whole;" his or her life is "put together;" everything is working together harmoniously in the person's life. People with integrity have nothing to hide and fear because their lives are like an open book. In other words, they are *integers.*

(F) *Shepherding Demands a Heart of Obedience:* This is the attitude of the heart of the leader towards higher authority. As Christians, the foremost higher authority is God Himself. The Lord said in John 14:15, *"If you love me, keep my commandments."* Obedience also deals with the individual's own attitude toward God. Apostle Paul thought he was working for the Lord while he was killing Christians, but when he encountered Jesus, he surrendered to His Lordship, and unreservedly chose to obey Him. In Acts 22:10, Apostle Paul states:

"I asked, 'What should I do, Lord?' and the Lord told me, 'Get up and go into Damascus, and there you will be told everything you are to do.'"

Paul's first order when he encountered the Master was: *"Now get up and go into the city, and you will be told what you must do."* (Acts 9:6). Paul had a choice – to obey or not to obey. Obedience is a part of the profile that made Paul a powerful man of influence.

You must search yourself and ask if there are any areas of disobedience in your life that you need to deal with? I do earnestly ask you to give it up! Hand them over to God, else, your growth will be truncated, and you may end up in frustration!

Other obedient men were Abraham, Moses and Daniel. God asked Abraham to sacrifice his only son (Genesis 22:2), and he obeyed. He asked Moses to confront Pharaoh and lead God's people out of Egypt (Exodus 3:10), and he obeyed God. Nebuchadnezzar's men told Daniel to stop worshipping God or be thrown into the lion's den (Daniel 6:8-17), but he obeyed God instead.

Dear friend, God asked each of these men to do something. God asked Paul to **get up**, He asked Abraham to **give up,** God asked Moses to **speak up** and He asked Daniel to **stand up**. Is God asking for your obedience in any of these ways? Is He is asking you to *get up out of your La-Z-Boy chair* and be more involved with your family or church?

Is there something that God is asking you to *give up— something you love* that is standing between you and complete obedience and service to God? Or are there some people – or some *issues – God would have you speak up to as a witness* about the things of God? Or are there some *practices in your family or at work that you should stand up to,* or take a stand against? When we follow God in obedience, you and I will join the ranks of the great men in the Bible.

We live in critical days and we cannot afford to waste our strength and/or our time. The Body of Christ desperately needs us to be more efficient in the ministry that God has given us.

The Bible says in Proverbs 27:17, NIV that, *Iron sharpens Iron, so one man sharpens another.* We must all be motivated and prepared to spend the time and make the effort to sharpen our skills.

Chapter Seven

Responsibilities of a Spiritual Leader

～

Care for the flock that God has entrusted to you. Watch over it willingly, not grudgingly – not for what you will get out of it, but because you are eager to serve God. ³ Don't lord it over the people assigned to your care, but lead them by your own good example.

(1 Peter 5:2-3)

I saw the phrases below in the blogosphere and they ministered life to me.[1] The phrases helped to form a background for writing this chapter. The phrases dealt with the responsibilities of a leader.

1. The modern leader (preacher) does not lack intellectuality, he lacks spirituality.
2. The modern leader (preacher) does not lack learning, he lacks burning.
3. The modern leader (preacher) has too much society, not enough solitude.

---

[1] http://www.city-data.com/forum/christianity/1045035- modern-preachers.html

4. He is too much with the people, and not enough with God.
5. He rings door bells well, but knocks but little at the door of Heaven.
6. He answers many telephone calls, but at the expense of a connection with Heaven.
7. He does not belong to the "Kneeling Order".

So get rid of all the filth and evil in your lives, and humbly accept the word God has planted in your hearts, for it has the power to save your souls.

(James 1:21, KJV)

Responsibility is the quality or state of being responsible such as a moral, legal, or mental accountability.

There is a lot of difference between *"a profession"* and *"a calling"*. Let me explain what I mean. Suppose there is a sick child in a hospital and a nurse looks after her for eight hours on her shift-duty. That nurse then goes home and forgets all about that child. Her concern for that child was only for eight hours.

Now she has other things to do, such as going to the movies and watching television. She does not have to think about that child again until the next day when she goes back to work. But the mother of that child does not work 8-hour shifts. She can't go to the movies when her child is sick. That is the difference between a profession and a calling.

If you apply that illustration to the way you care for the believers in your church, group or home cell, you will discover whether you are a *nurse* or a *mother!*

Apostle Paul said, in 1 Thessalonians 2:7-8;

*As apostles of Christ we certainly had a right to make some demands of you, but instead we were like children among you. Or we were like a **mother** feeding and caring for her own children. [8] We loved you so much that we shared with you not only God's Good News but our own lives, too.*

In Paul's letters to Timothy as shown in 2 Timothy 2:1-7, 15, 20-21, 24-26 (NLT), he used the synonyms to describe a leader and their respective tasks or responsibilities:

*Timothy, my dear son, be strong through the grace that God gives you in Christ Jesus. [2]You have heard me teach things that have been confirmed by many reliable witnesses. Now teach these truths to other **trustworthy people** who will be able to **pass them on to others**. [3] **Endure suffering** along with me, as a **good soldier** of Christ Jesus. [4] Soldiers don't get tied up in the affairs of civilian life, for then they cannot please the officer who enlisted them. [5] And **athletes** cannot win the prize unless they **follow the rules.** [6] And **hardworking farmers** should be the first to enjoy the fruit of their labor. [7] Think about what I am saying. The Lord **will help you understand** all these things. [15]Work hard so you can present yourself to God and receive his approval. Be **a good worker,** one who does not need to be ashamed and who **correctly explains the word** of truth. [20]In a wealthy home some **utensils are made of gold** and silver, and some are made of wood and clay. The expensive utensils are used for special occasions, and the cheap ones are for everyday use. [21] If you keep yourself **pure,** you will be a special **utensil for honorable** use. Your life will be **clean,** and you will be ready for the Master to use you for every*

good work. *²⁴A servant of the Lord must not quarrel but must be **kind to everyone**, be able to teach, and be patient with difficult people. ²⁵**Gently** instruct those who oppose the truth. Perhaps God will change those people's hearts, and they will learn the truth. ²⁶Then they will come to their senses and escape from the devil's trap. For they have been held captive by him to do whatever he wants.*

1. TRAINER

As trainer-leaders, we are to train and equip faithful men in what we have been commissioned to get done so as to be qualified to pass on the baton and train/teach others as well.

2. SOLDIER

Soldiers naturally are to endure hardship and to focus on their mission in order to accomplish it so that the He who has enrolled them into the Kingdom Army of the Lord may be pleased (Verse 3-4).

3. ATHLETE

Discipline and integrity are essential ingredients in leadership. A leader that lacks integrity and discipline cannot disciple others in faith and lawfulness because those he intends to lead will be corrupted and will not abide by the law of the race (Heavenly race) (Verse 5).

4. FARMER

Leaders are encouraged to work as farmers: growing the people in their care. As a leader willing to develop other leaders, cultivating, cherishing and receiving them in the way of the Lord should precede the act of developmental processes (Verse 6-7).

5. WORKER

Verse 15 clearly describes ways that potential leaders are to handle God's word accurately. Evidently, the central thought of this expression is the approving of ourselves to God, not to men. It is proper enough that we should have the approval of all good men and women. However, our primary goal is not to please men as mentioned above but to please God ultimately. In other words, we should aspire to please God and be approved of Him. One could notice that there is a contemplative study, such as David speaks of in Psalm 119:15 thus: *I meditate upon thy law day and night.* To see how that law would work out, its height and depth, its length and breadth of influence upon him. And so the Apostle's thought here is that it should be our chief aim to please God. We are to study and labor to handle God's Word accurately.

6. VESSEL

We are to stay pure so that God can use us for His highest purposes. In verses 20-21: Holiness must be the minimum standard for God's highest purpose to be fulfilled in the lives of both the leader and the potential leader. Sanctification and setting-aside for the Lord's use should also be the watchword for any leader in His Vineyard. *And meet for the master's use, useful for the master, fit in the spirit and character for service, prepared unto, for every good work, made ready the Holy Spirit in Christian virtues and graces to engage in every good work that may cone to hand. The idea here is of a real, genuine separation, a full consecration, and the needed spiritual preparation for Christian work.* That is to say every leader must be noble and fully Christ-like in words and deeds.

47

7. BONDSERVANT

We are to submit and stay humble, being kind to all people. Submission, humility and kindness must be the watchword for spiritual leaders. An example was Moses, a spiritual leader that will keep watch over the souls in his flock, knowing full well that he has to give an account to God one day for each of them.

Obey your spiritual leaders, and do what they say. Their work is to watch over your souls, and they are accountable to God. Give them reason to do this with joy and not with sorrow. That would certainly not be for your benefit.

(Hebrews 13:17)

Seven Changes Moses Made to Assume His Responsibility as a Leader:

1. He became a man of PRAYER

Now listen to me, and let me give you a word of advice, and may God be with you. You should continue to be the people's representative before God, bringing their disputes to him.

(Exodus 18:19)

2. He committed himself to COMMUNICATION

Teach them *God's decrees, and give them his instructions. Show them how to conduct their lives.*

(Exodus 18:20)

3. He laid out the VISION

*Teach them God's decrees, and **give them his instructions.** Show them how to conduct their lives.*

(Exodus 18:20)

4. He developed a **PLAN**

   Teach them God's decrees, and give them his instructions. **Show them** *how to conduct their lives.*

   (Exodus 18:20)

5. He **SELECTED** and trained the leaders

   But select *from all the people* **some capable, honest men** *who fear God and hate bribes. Appoint them as leaders over groups of one thousand, one hundred, fifty, and ten.*

   (Exodus 18:21)

6. He released them to **SERVE** based on their gifts

   Have them serve as judges for the people at all times, but have them bring every difficult case to you; the **simple cases they can decide themselves.**

   (Exodus 18:21a)

7. He only did what **THEY** could not do

   That will make your load lighter, because they will share it with you.

   (Exodus 18:21b)

In Exodus 18:23, we see the results of Moses' change: strength for Moses and peace for the people. *"If you do this thing, and God so commands you, then you will be able to endure, and this entire people will also go to their place in peace."*

49

THE TASKS OF A LEADER

Potential leaders will do the following things:

1. **INFLUENCE OTHERS**

   This is the most consistent fact about leaders. Note who they influence, how many they influence, and when they influence others.

2. **CHALLENGE THE PROCESS**

   They are hungry to make things better and are willing to effect change. They enjoy making progress and become restless when things remain static.

3. **BE DRIVEN BY A VISION**

   They can get others excited about their dreams; and the person with a vision talks little but does a lot. They have a fire inside of them to fulfill their dreams.

4. **RELATE WELL WITH PEOPLE**

   Leaders will not experience long-term success unless a lot of people support them. Potential leaders have learned the value of people and can connect with them.

5. **WORK WELL UNDER PRESSURE**

   Their value lies in what they can do and what they can endure. You will notice that potential leaders have the ability to thrive under pressure.

6. **SOLVE PROBLEMS WELL**

   You can judge a leader by the magnitude of the problems he handles. In other words, people almost always encounter problems they may be able to solve.

7. **COMMUNICATE EFFECTIVELY**

When leaders communicate, they make people to think, feel and act differently.

WHAT DID JESUS DO AS A LEADER?

In Luke 9:1-2, the Bible states

"One day Jesus called together his twelve disciples and gave them power and authority to cast out all demons and to heal all diseases. ² Then he sent them out to tell everyone about the Kingdom of God and to heal the sick."

We see in this passage that Jesus shared both responsibility and authority. To succeed in our mission, we must share both our work and power with a team. Jesus aimed to develop the disciples as He shared the work. He did not spend the majority of His time with the masses. Rather, he focused on training the disciples. By not spending equal time with everyone, but more time with those who were ready to be trained (A and B teams), Jesus was able to multiply His ministry in about three years.

The Developmental Process may be summarized as follows:

1. I do it while you watch
2. We do it together
3. You do it while I watch
4. We evaluate
5. You do it while another watches

Remember, it's not about you!

Once upon a time, there were these farmyard animals that gave a report at the end of the day about their days' activities. All the animals gathered together in the barn, and the rooster said: "I was up before everybody else, announcing the new day." Then the cow gave the report about how she "faithfully supplied the farmer with milk." One after the other, they shared about the day's events.

Meanwhile, the donkey waited patiently and paced back and forth. Finally it was his turn and he exclaimed, "You won't believe my day. This was the greatest day in my life! I wish you'd have been there to see me. I still can't get over what happened." Everyone listened in amazement as he narrated his report thus: "Today I walked down the main road of Jerusalem. Thousands upon thousands of people were there lining the road. They had their palm branches and were waving them at me and crying out, 'Hosanna, hosanna.' Oh, I mean, it was incredible. I felt so loved, so adored, and so important. I'll never forget this day as long as I live."

The problem in this story is "the donkey forgot about who was riding on his back." However, humanly speaking, if care is not taken, we begin to think that it's all about us and what we've done. We forgot that without Him, we can do nothing, absolutely nothing. We take the glory so readily, don't we? We begin to feel that we are just a little better than somebody else proud. Remember Nebuchadnezzar in Daniel 4:30-33:

> *As he looked out across the city, he said, "Look at this great city of Babylon! By my own mighty power, I have built this beautiful city as my royal residence to display*

my majestic splendor."[31] While these words were still in his mouth, a voice called down from heaven, "O King Nebuchadnezzar, this message is for you! You are no longer ruler of this kingdom. [32] You will be driven from human society. You will live in the fields with the wild animals, and you will eat grass like a cow. Seven periods of time will pass while you live this way, until you learn that the Most High rules over the kingdoms of the world and gives them to anyone he chooses."[33] That same hour the judgment was fulfilled, and Nebuchadnezzar was driven from human society. He ate grass like a cow, and he was drenched with the dew of heaven. He lived this way until his hair was as long as eagles' feathers and his nails were like birds' claws.

This passage indicates that his sovereignty was taken away and he was driven out of the palace to be among the beasts of the field until he recognized that God will not share His Glory with any man, not even Kings of this world.

THE SEVEN DEADLY SIPHONS
(Reasons we lose enthusiasm)

Loss of spiritual passion seems to be the inevitable result of some inherent phenomena; some of such are mentioned as follows.

1. **Words without action**: We are tempted to think that saying something actualizes it. We have a momentary feeling of spirituality when we talk about wanting to pray more or "have more time in the Word."

> *Work brings profit, but mere talk leads to poverty!*
>
> **(Proverbs 14:23, ASV)**

2. **Busyness without purpose**: Ministry produces activities, programs, and conversations. If our choices of time-use are not disciplined by call and purpose, our energies become like a lazy, shallow river.

3. **Calendars without a Sabbath**: A datebook filled with appointments but absent of significant hours (days) of quiet and reflection – written in first – is an abomination (an old and harsh word) to the God of the Bible, who said;

> *You have six days each week for your ordinary work, but the seventh day must be a Sabbath day of complete rest, a holy day dedicated to the Lord. Anyone who works on the Sabbath must be put to death.*
>
> **(Exodus 31:15)**

4. **Relationships without mutual nourishment**: Pastors tend to be acquainted with too many people but know too few people. The spiritual masters have told us for centuries that without soul-friends, we won't gain spiritual momentum.

5. **Pastoral personality without self-examination**: Too much ministry is built on unresolved anger, unhealthy needs for approval, and the instinct to control. Failing to explore our soul for un-wholeness ultimately takes its toll.

6. **Natural giftedness without spiritual power**: A Pastor can go a considerable distance in ministry with

catchy words, people skills, political savvy, and a facility for organizational dynamics. But kingdom work demands qualities that only a *filled-up* soul can offer.

7. **An enormous theology without an adequate spirituality**: A Pastor cannot represent a view of reality that includes creation, evil, reconciliation and conversion, sacrificial service, and eternity – a mind-boggling expanse of conviction – and have a spiritual exercise regimen that is pea-size in contrast. "A great theology demands a great spirituality" (Gordon MacDonald).

Chapter Eight
The Battle Axe for the Lord

∽

GOD'S WEAPON

And all of this is a gift from God, who brought us back to himself through Christ. And God has given us this task of reconciling people to him.

(2 Corinthians 5:18)

The Lord's purpose and uttermost desire for us (believers) is to be His battle axe, causing havoc on the kingdom of darkness and pulling down its strongholds.

"You are my battle-ax and sword," says the Lord. "With you I will shatter nations and destroy many kingdoms."

(Jeremiah 51:20)

We are God's battle axe to wreak havoc on the kingdom of Satan. Not only for us to be a battle axe, we also need to be purged, so that we can always be ready when occasion demands.

"Son of man, give the people this message from the Lord: A sword, a sword is being sharpened and polished.¹⁰ It is

> *sharpened for terrible slaughter and polished to flash like lightning! Now will you laugh? Those far stronger than you have fallen beneath its power!"*
>
> **(Ezekiel 21:9-10a)**

Dear friends, you are the swords God has chosen to sharpen for this great end time work. I pray you will not be found wanting in the name of Jesus.

> *Using a dull ax requires great strength, so sharpen your blade. That's the value of wisdom; it helps you succeed.*
>
> **(Ecclesiastes 10:10)**

We live in critical days and we cannot afford to waste strength and time. The Lord is now sharpening those whom He will use in these last days for that great battle of the ages. The Body of Christ urgently needs individual Christians who are pliable in the hands of God, so that they can be efficient in the ministry God has called them.

"There is no sudden leap into the stratosphere. There is only advancing step by step, slowly and torturously, up the pyramid toward your goals." (Ben Stein)

There is nothing like instant success, except in your imagination. Winston Churchill once said, "If asked to chop down trees for 8 hours, he will use first six hours in sharpening the axe." (My emphasis) That of course, places emphasis on preparation before success.

CHARACTERISTICS OF BATTLE AXES

1. Called by God to be Battle Axes

God has declared us as His battle axe and weapons of war in Jeremiah 51:20 and our functionality is depicted in Ezekiel 21:9.

1a. God gave humans authority over the whole earth: Man needs to be comfortable with two positions; under God's authority and, the second, being in authority over the world.

Then God said, "Let us make human beings in our image, to be like us. They will reign over the fish in the sea, the birds in the sky, the livestock, all the wild animals on the earth, and the small animals that scurry along the ground."

(Genesis 1:26)

1b. If God told us we are battle axes, we must have the ability to do it because we have *The Enabler* in us.

In fact, this has happened here in this very city! For Herod Antipas, Pontius Pilate the governor, the Gentiles, and the people of Israel were all united against Jesus, your holy servant, whom you anointed. [28] But everything they did was determined beforehand according to your will. [29] And now, O Lord, hear their threats, and give us, your servants, great boldness in preaching your word. [30] Stretch out your hand with healing power; may miraculous signs and wonders be done through the name of your holy servant Jesus. [31] After this prayer, the meeting place shook, and they were all filled with the Holy Spirit. Then they preached the word of God with boldness.

(Acts 4:27-31, NIV)

God confirms the calling to influence others in **Matthew 5:13-16** that *we are the salt of the earth... the light of the world. "You are the light of the world – like a city on a hilltop that cannot be hidden."* Salt influences the food we eat, light influences the homes in which we live. We need to embrace our calling because our lives shine among our fellow men as we influence them for the cause of Christ. Therefore, in Isaiah 60:1, the Bible in a form of an assertion commands thus:

> *Arise, Jerusalem! Let your light shine for all to see. For the glory of the Lord rises to shine on you.*

(Isaiah 60:1)

2. Battle Axes are men and women of prayer

> *One day Jesus told his disciples a story to show that they should always pray and never give up.*

(Luke 18:1)

The Lord's battle axes understand the pivotal role of prayer and pray strategically during key times. They do not panic or fear because they *pray without ceasing* (1 Thessalonians 5:17).

Types of Prayer

2a. Prayer of Agreement: This kind of prayer is prayed according to **Matthew 18:18-20**, when two or more people pray in agreement, the power generated is multiplied as a result.

> *"I tell you the truth, whatever you forbid on earth will be*

forbidden in heaven, and whatever you permit on earth will be permitted in heaven. [19] I also tell you this: If two of you agree here on earth concerning anything you ask, my Father in heaven will do it for you. [20] For where two or three gather together as my followers, I am there among them."

2b. Prayer of Petition: This is a type of prayer we are most familiar with. In it we ask God for things we need – primarily spiritual needs, but physical ones as well.

"I tell you, you can pray for anything, and if you believe that you've received it, it will be yours."

(Mark 11:24)

2c. Prayer of Thanksgiving: This is a kind of prayer where we thank God for all the wonderful things He does for us; favor, mercy, loving-kindness, grace, long-suffering and goodness. For example, thanksgiving is illustrated in Philippians 4:6:

Don't worry about anything; instead, pray about everything. Tell God what you need, and thank him for all he has done.

2d. Prayer of Intercession: This is to be offered on behalf of other people – your friends, family, co-workers, and so on. Do those around you have needs, concerns, or health problems? If so, cry *out* to God on their behalf. For instance, Ezekiel 22:30 states that,

"I looked for someone who might rebuild the wall of righteousness that guards the land. I searched for someone to stand in the gap in the wall so I wouldn't have to destroy the land, but I found no one."

2e. Prayer of Commitment: There is no way we can be victorious, apart from trusting God with our lives. The prayer of commitment brings us greater freedom because we are handing over our burdens to God. This prayer should be prayed often remembering that nothing is too big or too small to pray about – pray about everything. In 1 Peter 5:7, the Word of God encourages you to *Give all your worries and cares to God, for he cares about you.* It goes further in Proverbs 16:3 to assert thus: *Commit your actions to the L*ord*, and your plans will succeed.*

2f. Prayer of Consecration: We pray this kind of prayer when we surrender our lives to the Lordship of Jesus Christ, and ask that His will be done. In other words, Acts. 9:6 places more emphasis on how committed we should be in asking God what he wants us to do thus: *So he, trembling and astonished, said, "Lord, what do You want me to do?" Then the Lord said to him, "Now get up and go into the city, and you will be told what you must do."*

Levels of Prayer

During times of war, we hear the military terms like logistical, tactical and strategic initiatives. While these terms describe three levels of military operations, they also describe three levels of prayer.

i. Logistical Prayer: In this type of prayer, the focus is on personal need – temporal perspective. Such prayers may sound like,

"Lord, help us to do well this morning. Help us to finish our service on time, make the microphone function well and help us to be calm, Amen."

ii. **Tactical Prayer:** The focus of this is on helping others, but still from a temporal perspective.

"Lord, please bless all who participate in the service today, and bless the people who attend. Let it be inspiring to everyone, Amen."

Better, but still does not fully capture God's heart and purpose for the world.

iii. **Strategic prayer:** The focus is on God's ultimate objective for the world. These are prayers prayed from an eternal perspective.

"Lord, raise up disciples from this service today. Regardless of what happens to the microphones, the musicians or anyone else on the platform, use this service to glorify Yourself and bring your kingdom more fully to this earth, Amen."

The story in *2 **Kings** 3:5-10* is illustrative at this point.

> *But after Ahab's death, the king of Moab rebelled against the king of Israel.* ⁶ *So King Joram promptly mustered the army of Israel and marched from Samaria.* ⁷ *On the way, he sent this message to King Jehoshaphat of Judah: "The king of Moab has rebelled against me. Will you join me in battle against him?" And Jehoshaphat replied, "Why, of course! You and I are as one. My troops are your troops, and my horses are your horses."* ⁸ *Then Jehoshaphat asked, "What route will we take?" "We will attack from the wilderness of Edom," Joram replied.* ⁹ *The king of Edom and his troops joined them, and all three armies traveled along a roundabout route through the wilderness for seven days. But there was no water for*

> *the men or their animals.[10] "What should we do?" the*
> *king of Israel cried out. "The Lord has brought the three*
> *of us here to let the king of Moab defeat us."*

Before the army of Israel faced the Moabites in battle, they ran out of water. They went to Elijah to seek God's help for water. God responded that He will give them water, but it was a small task for Him. In addition to that, He promised to give the Moabite into their hands. Israel asked for the wrong thing – water, not the war! It is my prayer that your meditation and your asking will be ordered aright in the name of Jesus.

> *But giving thanks is a sacrifice that truly honors me. If*
> *you keep to my path, I will reveal to you the salvation*
> *of God.*

(Psalm 50:23)

3. Battle axes are effective communicators

Proverbs 15:23 states that *Everyone enjoys a fitting reply; it is wonderful to say the right thing at the right time!* In other words, spoken words are magical and could do wonders even beyond our wildest imagination. A great example is a speech given by Martin Luther King Jr. in the 20th century. The famous speech probably was not made by a politician, business leader, or Hollywood celebrity. It was made by a Pastor. In 1963, Dr. Martin Luther King, Jr. stood on the steps of the Lincoln memorial and delivered a six-minute memorable speech.

After finishing his planned words, King spoke from the depth of his heart and connected with over 100,000 people and countless others via television. A masterful communicator, repeating one phrase over and over, "I have a dream!" by the time he finished, he had cast a clear vision. His words had created a movement. So also are the words of Elijah when he wanted to demonstrate to the people and to the world the glory and the supremacy of God as it is depicted in 1 Kings 18:30:

> *Then Elijah called to the people, "Come over here!" They all crowded around him as he repaired the altar of the Lord that had been torn down.*

However, When Elijah spoke, the people were amazed. But most amazing of all was that by the end of the day after all the theatrics, Elijah turned his face toward heaven and cried 1 Kings 18:37 thus:

> *O Lord, answer me! Answer me so these people will know that you, O Lord, are God and that you have brought them back to yourself.*

And God answered.

What about our Lord Jesus Christ! What made Him such a great communicator? There's no doubt that He knew how to get His message across in a way that had a strong and lasting impact on many people. How He did it is illustrated in the Gospel of Matthew 13:3

3a. Simplifying the Message

> *Then He spoke many things to them in parables, saying: "Behold, a sower went out to sow;" His disciples came and asked him, "Why do you use parables when you talk to the people?"[1] He replied, "You are permitted to understand the secrets of the Kingdom of Heaven, but others are not. [12] To those who listen to my teaching,*

more understanding will be given, and they will have an abundance of knowledge. But for those who are not listening, even what little understanding they have will be taken away from them. ¹³ That is why I use these parables, For they look, but they don't really see. They hear, but they don't really listen or understand.¹⁴ This fulfills the prophecy of Isaiah that says, 'When you hear what I say, you will not understand. When you see what I do, you will not comprehend.

(Matthew 13:10-14)

It is not what you say, but how you say it. Jesus was not superficial, He was simple. He told stories everyone could relate to, simplifying the complicated!

3b. Seeing the Person

Later that same day Jesus left the house and sat beside the lake. ² A large crowd soon gathered around him, so he got into a boat. Then he sat there and taught as the people stood on the shore.

(Matthew 13:1-2)

It is not what you say, but how people see it. Jesus was faced with a large and varied audience. He knew them well enough to speak their language so that they could understand Him. At the end of the day, Jesus affirmatively stated:

"Anyone with ears to hear should listen and understand."

(Matthew 13:9)

3c. Seizing the Moment

It's not what you say, but when you say it. The Bible says in Proverbs 15:23b that, *a word spoken in due season, how good it is!* Jesus has an understanding of this and He spoke at the right time when the people came to hear Him.

A large crowd soon gathered around him, so he got into a boat. Then he sat there and taught as the people stood on the shore.

(Matthew 13:2)

He waited until they showed initiative. When they rejected His message, He withdrew. Right timing is paramount in every life's endeavor. Therefore, before you embark on any venture, it is imperative that you know the right timing.

This fulfills the prophecy of Isaiah that says, "When you hear what I say, you will not understand. When you see what I do, you will not comprehend."[15] For the hearts of these people are hardened, and their ears cannot hear and they have closed their eyes — so their eyes cannot see, and their ears cannot hear, and their hearts cannot understand, and they cannot turn to me and let me heal them. [16] But blessed are your eyes, because they see; and your ears, because they hear. [17] I tell you the truth, many prophets and righteous people longed to see what you see, but they didn't see it. And they longed to hear what you hear, but they didn't hear it.

(Matthew 13:14-17)

3d. Showing the Truth

It is not what you say, but how you show it. Jesus did not merely use words, rather, he demonstrated credibility with His life and miracles, and proved He could be trusted. Why did Jim and Tammy-Fay Baker lose their ministry? It was because their lives were not in accordance to what they preached.

3e. Seeking the Response

Jesus said to them, "Have you understood all these things?" They said to Him, "Yes, Lord." Do you understand all these things?" "Yes," they said, "we do."

(Matthew 13:51)

It's not what you say, but how your audience responds. I actually recommend for every leader and teacher to make use of this feedback principle. Jesus always gave people something new to think, feel and do.

Jesus and his disciples left Galilee and went up to the villages near Caesarea Philippi. As they were walking along, he asked them, "Who do people say I am?" [28] "Well," they replied, "some say John the Baptist, some say Elijah, and others say you are one of the other prophets." [29] Then he asked them, "But who do you say I am?" Peter replied, "You are the Messiah."

(Mark 8:27-29)

4.   Battle Axes have Character

Spiritual leadership is based on the work of the Holy Spirit and on spiritual character. Oswald Sanders asked, "Should it not be the office that seeks the man, rather than the man the office? Why are we shocked to hear about the Enron CEO's disaster? Why are we scandalized to discover that the Pastor of a mega church has committed adultery?

We have accepted the false assumption that those in high positions have achieved their status based on sound character – Wrong, wrong assumption! Gaining the position as the Pastor of a church does not make one Spirit-filled, graduating from Seminary does not make one a spiritual leader. Holding a leadership position in a Christian organization does not automatically come with God's anointing.

4a. Honesty

Employees have counted honesty in their leaders as more important than vision, competence, accomplishments, and the ability to inspire others. Henry Blackaby and Richard Blackaby (2011) defined integrity as "a firm attachment to moral or artistic principle; honesty and sincerity; uprightness; wholeness, completeness; the condition of being unmarred and uncorrupted, the original, perfect condition."

Integrity means being consistent in one's behavior under every circumstance, including those unguarded moments (Emotional self). Permit me to emphasize that integrity is doing the appropriate, even when nobody is watching.

4b. Integrity

Integrity is not automatic. It is a character trait that leaders consciously cultivate in their lives. Billy Graham was troubled by the notorious vices of well-known evangelists, and being aware, if not careful they too could fall prey to immorality. He led his group to identify those things most likely to destroy or hinder their ministry. They agreed upon a list of principles they would each follow in order to ensure integrity of their lives and ministry – to uphold the Bible standard of absolute integrity and purity. As a result, BGEA became foremost model on integrity for Christian organization the world ever knew. Integrity does not happen by accident, but on purpose.

4c. Obedience

The obedient needs only to obey. The Lord will not hold us responsible for any mistaken obedience; rather, He will hold the delegated authority responsible for his erroneous act. Insubordination is rebellion – for we all must answer to God. The rod of Saul's correction is not in the hand of David. For those who will want to pretend the ignorance of this, Samuel was not set to judge Eli. You should not venture into punishing the delegated authority over you.

Spiritual success is not defined in terms of ability. It is a matter of obedience. Joshua and Samuel are good examples of this fact.

> *Therefore, the Lord, the God of Israel, says: "I promised that your branch of the tribe of Levi would always be my priests. But I will honor those who honor me, and I will despise those who think lightly of me."*

(1 Samuel 2:30)

Henry Varley's challenging words could be relevant here: "Moody, the world has yet to see what God will do with a man fully consecrated to him." Moody was prepared to be that man, and God used him to become the greatest evangelist of the late-nineteenth century.

5. Battle Axes know that they can be disqualified, therefore they avoid pitfalls

Why is it that some leaders go from victory to victory, year after year, while other begins with great promise but eventually crash into oblivion? Certainly, they did not set out expecting to fail, but sadly, their failure can usually be traced to mistakes they could easily have avoided. The ten pitfalls of leadership are:

5a. Pride: Learn to take credit from others. Proverbs 27:2 **makes** it clear on how self-pride can diminish a man. Instead, let another person praise our good word:

> *Let someone else praise you, not your own mouth — a stranger, not your own lips.*

Another example self-pride is given by the narration of the story of Nebuchadnezzar who thought the whole world was under his authority in Daniel 4:29-32:

> *Twelve months later he was taking a walk on the flat roof of the royal palace in Babylon. [30] As he looked out across the city, he said, 'Look at this great city of Babylon! By my own mighty power, I have built this beautiful city as my royal residence to display my majestic splendor.' [31] "While these words were still in his mouth, a voice called down from heaven, 'O King Nebuchadnezzar, this message is for you! You are no longer ruler of this kingdom. [32] You will be driven from human society. You will live in the fields with the wild animals, and you will eat grass like a cow. Seven periods*

71

> *of time will pass while you live this way, until you learn that the Most High rules over the kingdoms of the world and gives them to anyone he chooses.*

Furthermore, we do not need to show that we are unteachable and self-sufficient like Samson because this attitude could be a function of a fatal end if we are not very careful.

5b. Sexual sin: The most insidious pitfall and the most notorious. Be accountable and develop safeguards.

5c. Cynicism: When leaders are constantly criticizing others, they are modeling a critical spirit for their people

5d. Greed: Why does God always seem to call ministers to churches that pay more money and never to churches that pay less? It is mostly a manifestation of greed in the ministers.

5e. Mental Laziness: Great leaders are always learning how to become better leaders. Readers are leaders. Additional learning is mandatory to keep a job.

5f. Oversensitivity: Oswald Sanders said, "Often the crowd does not recognize a leader until he has gone, and then they build a monument for him with stones they threw at him in life."

> *"But in that coming day no weapon turned against you will succeed. You will silence every voice raised up to accuse you. These benefits are enjoyed by the servants of the Lord; their vindication will come from me. I, the Lord, have spoken!"*
>
> **(Isaiah 54:17)**

5g. Spiritual Lethargy: Do not ever substitute your public prayer life for your personal conversations with God. Everyone that would be used of God needs to be alone with Him from time to time. It is important to realize that these are the times to receive instructions and directions.

5h. Domestic Neglect: Leaders who value their families seek for creative ways to make their jobs a blessing to their families instead of a rival for their attention. God is the family's biggest advocate.

5i. Administrative Carelessness: To have a testimony in ministry, a servant of God needs to develop the reputation of dealing with important issues promptly and thoroughly.

5j. Prolonged position holding: Hold everything loosely! Do not build empires! Do not behave as if you are already in your destination. Have a realization that the time spent in a position is a privilege and opportunity for training and exposure. Always look forward to what God will do next. And that is why Philippians 3:12-16 states:

> *I don't mean to say that I have already achieved these things or that I have already reached perfection. But I press on to possess that perfection for which Christ Jesus first possessed me. [13] No, dear brothers and sisters, I have not achieved it, but I focus on this one thing: Forgetting the past and looking forward to what lies ahead, [14] I press on to reach the end of the race and receive the heavenly prize for which God, through Christ Jesus, is calling us. [15] Let all who are spiritually mature*

> *agree on these things. If you disagree on some point, I believe God will make it plain to you.* [16] *But we must hold on to the progress we have already made.*

To avoid the pitfalls, develop a healthy awareness of the pitfalls. Put safeguards in place, put reminders in place, and involve competent people in your organization. Remember you are not indispensable, and maintain a close, vibrant relationship with God.

6. Battle Axes look after their Appearance

Many people underestimate how big an impact their appearance has on how others perceive them. We are all quick to judge others on how they look, but somehow we cannot believe that others are doing exactly the same to us. If you look after your physical appearance, you will go a long way towards having good charisma. Someone once said that, you are addressed the way you dress. Here are some simple suggestions on that point:

6a. Dress your best, always be conservative, and use modest clothing.

6b. Keep yourself clean, bathe daily, wash your hair once every few days, get your shoes polished, and clean your teeth twice a day.

6c. Keep yourself tidy. If you are a man, keep your facial, nasal, and ear hair well-shaved. If you are a woman do the same for visible body hair.

6d. Keep your hair neat, tidy and stylish.

6e. Dress well. Wear fashionable, well-fitting clothes,

always be conservative and in modest clothing. Make sure your clothes are clean, well ironed, and new enough not to be faded. Aim to dress a bit better than those around you.

6f. Be mindful of color combinations. You may seek the opinion of someone or your spouse about what colors go with which. Avoid repeating the same clothes in a particular program or place.

6g. Lose bad smells. Wear deodorant and or perfume, but do not overdo it, subtle is the key. If you eat something spicy, drink coffee, or smoke, have a packet of mints handy to clear your breath afterwards.

6h. From the inside, take the time to lessen any negative feelings you may have about the upcoming encounter. List some positive aspects and focus on those. Negative emotions show up in your facial expressions and can actually make you look unattractive.

Appearance has been found to play a vital role in placements and appointments. In fact the Christians of to-day want to be sure of the charisma of whoever they call a leader.

But Samuel, though he was only a boy, served the Lord. He wore a linen garment like that of a priest.[19]*Each year his mother made a small coat for him and brought it to him when she came with her husband for the sacrifice.* [20]*Before they returned home, Eli would bless Elkanah and his wife and say, "May the Lord give you other children to take the place of this one she gave to the Lord"*

(1 Samuel 2:18-20)

> *And David danced before the Lord with all his might,*
> *wearing a priestly garment.*[15] *So David and all the people*
> *of Israel brought up the Ark of the Lord with shouts of*
> *joy and the blowing of rams' horns.*

(2 Samuel 6:14-15)

Brethren, do you know the reason why people dress well to interviews? It is because appearance commands favor? Esther's case is worthy of note:

> *On the third day of the fast, Esther put on her royal*
> *robes and entered the inner court of the palace, just across*
> *from the king's hall. The king was sitting on his royal*
> *throne, facing the entrance.* [2] *When he saw Queen Esther*
> *standing there in the inner court, he welcomed her and*
> *held out the gold scepter to her. So Esther approached*
> *and touched the end of the scepter.*

(Esther 5:1-2)

7. Battle Axes are Rewarded

For battle axes currently embroiled in the toil and stress of facing a major challenge, rewards can be encouraging.

> *And it is impossible to please God without faith. Anyone*
> *who wants to come to him must believe that God exists*
> *and that he rewards those who sincerely seek him.*

(Hebrews 11:6)

It is vital to note the following about rewards:

7a. The most tangible and obvious reward is monetary, however a stout bank balance does not always compensate for the pressure and criticism of leaders.

7b. They also enjoy the authority their position affords them, nevertheless, the reward of wealth, power and fame comes with accountability.

7c. Spiritual reward is very important too. No reward could possibly equal the joy that comes from knowing that the Almighty is pleased with you.

*And the Holy Spirit, in bodily form, descended on him like a dove. And a voice from heaven said, "You are my dearly loved Son, **and you bring me great joy.**"*

(Luke 3:22)

*The moment you began praying, a command was given. And now I am here to tell you what it was, for **you are very precious to God.** Listen carefully so that you can understand the meaning of your vision.*

(Daniel 9:23)

*Then the Lord asked Satan, "Have you noticed my servant Job? **He is the finest man** in all the earth. He is blameless – a man of complete integrity. He fears God and stays away from evil."*

(Job 1:8)

*Then the Lord asked Satan, "Have you noticed my servant Job? He is the finest man in all the earth. **He is blameless – a man of complete integrity.** He fears God and stays away from evil. And he has **maintained his integrity**, even though you urged me to harm him without cause."*

(Job 2:3)

7d. The satisfaction of knowing you have accomplished God's will and purposes for your life, and have reached your maximum potential in life is gratifying to the soul.

> *... I obeyed that vision from heaven*

(Acts 26:19)

Apostle Paul, a man of purpose said;

> *I press on to reach the end of the race and receive the heavenly prize for which God, through Christ Jesus, is calling us.*

(Philippians 3:14)

> *I have fought the good fight, I have finished the race, and I have remained faithful. And now the prize awaits me — the crown of righteousness, which the Lord, the righteous Judge, will give me on the day of his return. And the prize is not just for me but for all who eagerly look forward to his appearing.*

(2 Timothy 4:7-8)

In John 19: 29-30, the word of God states thus:

> *A jar of sour wine was sitting there, so they soaked a sponge in it, put it on a hyssop branch, and held it up to his lips. [30] When Jesus had tasted it, he said, "It is finished!" Then he bowed his head and released his spirit.*

7e. The ability to look people in the eye and know that you have nothing, for which you ought to be ashamed of, is a record of inestimable value.

Samuel was bold to say to all the Israelites;

> *Now testify against me in the presence of the Lord and before his anointed one. Whose ox or donkey have I stolen? Have I ever cheated any of you? Have I ever oppressed you? Have I ever taken a bribe and perverted justice? Tell me and I will make right whatever I have done wrong." "No," they replied, "you have never cheated or oppressed us, and you have never taken even a single bribe."*

(1 Samuel 12:3-4)

Jesus also declared:

> *"I don't have much more time to talk to you, because the ruler of this world approaches. He has no power over me, ...*

(John 14:30)

8.   Battle Axes walk Alone

The plan and the purpose of God for our lives is that we conform to the image of His Son. It is a slow work and walk. So slow that it takes God all of time and eternity to make a man or woman conform. Part of the process of being a battle axe is to allow Him to show us the deep, hidden areas of our own character. It is astounding how ignorant we are about ourselves. We do not even recognize the envy, laziness, pride, self-conceit, intellectual pride, misplaced affections within us. Therefore, areas of stubbornness and ignorance will be dealt with when Jesus isolates us from others.

8a. Daniel alone saw the vision (of the post incarnate Christ).

> *Only I, Daniel, saw this vision. The men with me saw nothing, but they were suddenly terrified and ran away to hide. He will bring me glory by telling you whatever he receives from me.* ¹⁵ *All that belongs to the Father is mine; this is why I said, 'The Spirit will tell you whatever he receives from me.'*

(John 16:14-15)

8b. Paul alone saw the vision on the road to Damascus (Acts 9:7,8), and after that, He had two years of solitary confinement on that same desert, for God to train him.

8c. Abraham left Ur, and finally his kindred, and he was alone with God.

8d. Moses was sent to the backside of the desert of Midian, saw the burning bush alone (Exodus 3:1-3).

8e. Elijah was disciplined by the *Brook Cherith* alone, but God was with him (1 Kings 17:2-5).

8f. Jeremiah walked a lonely path.

8g. John the Baptist was alone in the desert (Luke 1:80).

8h. Apostle John was exiled on the lonely isle of Patmos alone (Revelations 1:9).

Separate yourself from the busyness of life and take time out to seek God. As you do that consistently, He will impart you with His glory, so that you can be a great blessing to your generation and generations yet unborn.

Battle axes are very noble in all their undertakings, but it must be something God has to assign for us to work hand in hand with the Holy Spirit. The work of the kingdom is not something we can do by mere zeal; we need the *grace of God*. God is enlisting people and preparing them for the end time harvest. If you want to be part of this great move of God, sing this song and pray the prayers below with all your heart:

Fill my cup Lord I lift it up Lord
Come and quench this thirsting of my soul
Bread of heaven, feed me till I want no more
Fill my cup fill it up and make me whole

PRAYER POINTS

- Almighty God, let the Spirit of the battle axe come upon me, my home and ministry in Jesus' name.

- Father! Sharpen me for your work here on earth in Jesus' name.

- Father! Let me excel as I walk with you in the name of Jesus.

- Daddy! Keep me focused that I may finish strong in the name of Jesus.

- Almighty God, fill my *Spiritual* cup to the glory of your holy name.

- I receive the boldness of God today as I move on in ministry and life in Jesus' name.

Chapter Nine

The Mature Man

⌁

Before you are allowed to get a driver's license in the United States, you have to demonstrate a certain level of competence. You will have to demonstrate a working knowledge of road signs and show that you are able to read and respond to them appropriately. These signs are so important that people who designed them, make them clear enough that you do not even need words to express their meanings. For example, a "U" inside a red circle with a line running through means no U-turns.

Two lines joining together to form a single line that terminates in an arrow connotes that two lanes are merging to form one. Also if you see the number "55"; that means the speed limit in that area is 55 miles per hour. One general idea behind road signs is that, it is possible, at least in theory, to always know what you should be doing behind the wheel. The sign makers seek to eliminate the guesswork. One sometimes thinks: *"Wouldn't it be nice if they didn't just have signs for roads but also had signs for people too?"*

Relational Education

Just consider the following with an objective mind:

- You come to work, and there's a big sign around your boss' neck: "Had huge fight with my spouse this morning – proceed with caution."

- You go to tuck your child in late at night, and you're tired and tempted to rush the moment, when you see the sign: "Growing up too fast – reduce speed."

- You go out on a date with someone you don't know very well, and then you see a sign, "Severely and breathtakingly dysfunctional – run for your life. Backing up will cause severe tire damage."

- I have PMS – run for your life!

Maybe it would be better if we all had to take "relationship education" in school, the way we take driver's education and had to be licensed before we could start navigating relationships on our own? Would it not be a lot better if people are pulled over by *"relationship police"* for such things as talking too fast, talking too long, talking too loud, failure to come to a complete and thoughtful "stop" before executing a proper confrontation, trying to merge when all signs said "road closed."

In the real spiritual sense of it, we have relational signs for human beings; the sad thing is that we do not learn to read them.

> *The lamp of the Lord searches the spirit of a person; it searches out the inmost being.*

84

The Lord's light penetrates the human spirit, exposing every hidden motive.

(Proverbs 20:27, NIV)

For example, the Psalmist states:

You see me when I travel and when I rest at home. You know everything I do. You know what I am going to say even before I say it, Lord. You go before me and follow me. You place your hand of blessing on my head.

(Psalm 139:3-5)

This I call Maturity!

Job (A Real Man Among Men)

America (our State, community, neighborhood, and even church) is desperate for real heroes. From the world of entertainment to the sphere of politics, there is a lack of examples of true manhood. Where are those men that we can emulate and follow? Where are the people with courage, integrity, and virtue?

Where do we turn for such examples? There was such a man in history among men that was of great spiritual stature, and integrity, that had strong family values. His name was Job. Job is a real hero. It happened that in times of severe adversity, he did not abandon his integrity, virtue, and commitment to his family and to his God.

Let us look at seven Biblical traits of Masculinity (Real Men) from the life of Job.

1. Job Learned from the Past Experience

I long for the years gone by when God took care of me, when he lit up the way before me and I walked safely through the darkness. When I was in my prime, God's friendship was felt in my home. The Almighty was still with me, and my children were around me. My cows produced milk in abundance, and my groves poured out streams of olive oil.

(Job 29:2-6)

Job was remembering his past glorious days. He valued the past, but not as one who yearns for "the good old days" in order to keep them from dealing with the present reality. Rather, he valued the past because of the truth it taught him about God, about people, and about himself, just in reminiscence of Proverbs 22:28, which says *do not remove the ancient landmark which your fathers have set.* By remembering how God had dealt with him in the past, Job was able to endure his present suffering.

What a contrast to modern day believers. Unlike Job, the man of today acts as if he has no past from which to learn. In fact, he has a subtle contempt for the past. We are even rewriting our history books, as if there were nothing in the past that we could learn from regarding today's issues. The question of the man of nowadays is: *"what's the economic advantage?"* As a people, we have made great scientific and technological strides in the last half of this Century.

This has lulled us into erroneous assumptions. Hence, the modern man's thoughts are thus illustrated:

- We must have made great improvements in human relationships.

- We need not look to the past for instructions on how to raise a family or how to be a man. Newer must be better. Unfortunately, even a brief glance at the headlines shows that in the realm of human relationships we are doing worse than those who went before us.

Marriages used to work, family members got along reasonably well. There was no talk of "alternative lifestyles" or even "divorce." Family members cared for each other and took responsibility for the actions of their siblings. Today, men seem to think that the past is outdated, old fashioned, and have no value for today's living. That is why no one values the Bible – they say "This is the 21st century..." We need to be real. Men today will never fully recapture their missing manhood until they repent of modern arrogance and humbly look at the history of God's definition of a real man. It ought to be realized that even the church is exhorted to maintain a link with the past.

Paul said to the Thessalonians:

> *Stand fast and hold to the traditions which you were taught, whether by word or our epistle. With all these things in mind, dear brothers and sisters, stand firm and keep a strong grip on the teaching we passed on to you both in person and by letter.*

(2 Thessalonians. 2:15)

2. Job Remained Close to His Children

Job remembers:

> *... And my children were around me.*
>
> **(Job 29:5b)**

The first part of the book of Job shows that he was a family man, a father to his children. It is interesting to note that in the midst of his suffering, Job said he missed having his children around him. He obviously did not view children as an intrusion into his personal pleasures. For example, in Psalm 127:5 states that:

> *How joyful is the man whose quiver is full of them! He will not be put to shame when he confronts his accusers at the city gates.*

And Psalm 128:3 also depicts thus:

> *Your wife shall be like a fruitful vine in the very heart of your house, Your children like olive plants All around your table. Your wife will be like a fruitful grapevine, flourishing within your home. Your children will be like vigorous young olive trees as they sit around your table.*

This is a contrast with many fathers today. Fathers have abandoned their children for their own personal pleasures. Children are viewed as a burden or a robber of money and time that could be used for personal pleasures. Many men have abandoned their role as fathers, leaving the women to raise the children themselves.

It is this selfish attitude that has increased child abuse, abortion, and other atrocities perpetrated against our children.

In **Job 1:5** we learn that Job:

> *(for his children)* [Emphasis Mine]
>
> *...would get up early in the morning and offer a burnt offering for each of them.*

For he said:

> *"Perhaps my children have sinned and have cursed God in their hearts."*

Job was worried that his kids would forget God, so he interceded for them. Job had ten children, yet, he took pains to be intimately involved in the physical and spiritual care of each of his seven sons and three daughters because he knew his responsibilities as a father that ever desired his children to follow the ways of God. This is portrayed in Proverbs 22:6, *Train up a child in the way he should go, And when he is old he will not depart from it.* In other words, one truth we cannot escape is that we are responsible for shaping the character of our children. To be the kind of father that Job was, we must crucify self and make our children a matter of our personal concern.

3. Job was a Respected Community Leader

> *Those were the days when I went to the city gate and took my place among the honored leaders. The young stepped aside when they saw me, and even the aged rose in respect at my coming. The princes stood in silence and put their hands over their mouths. The highest officials of the city stood quietly, holding their tongues in respect. "All who heard me praised me. All who saw me spoke well of me."*
>
> **(Job 29:7-11)**

The gate of the city was the place all the community leaders gathered and discussed the community affairs. Young men humbly withdrew and old men stood up to greet Job. This kind of respect comes the old fashioned way – it must be earned. Unfortunately, in today's world religious people have become notorious for their critical, judgmental speech. So we need men that speak God's truth in love.

Speaking it in such a way that shows respect to the person we are speaking to. We need to take a cue from what Apostle Peter said in 1 Peter 3:15: *Instead, you must worship Christ as Lord of your life. And if someone asks about your Christian hope, always be ready to explain it.* And what Paul did in Athens (Acts. 18:19): *While he was there, he went to the synagogue to reason with the Jews.*

Give a reason for your hope, not condemnation. Whenever Jesus condemned the religious leaders, He also gave a reason for the condemnation. Today's real heroes are concerned about community values, and the decline of public morals in our community, and are willing to express them in a kind but firm manner.

4. Job was a Father to the Fatherless

> *For I assisted the poor in their need and the orphans who required help. I helped those without hope, and they blessed me. And I caused the widows' hearts to sing for joy.*
>
> **(Job 29:12-13)**

Job was concerned with children and people beyond the needs of his own family. He was involved with the care and guidance of children whose families were not able to care for them. Job did not gather at the "Gate of the city" just to discuss matters but to act upon them! Today's youth need to see who is a real father – what a real man is like.

If we realize that a child's first impression of God is that of the image of a father, then we can see the importance of being a father to the children of the world. The world does not need any more men who use their children and families for their own selfish pursuits. The world needs men who unselfishly give themselves for the good of others – volunteer as basketball coach, etc. We need God's intervention if we are to come close to emulating Job to the world around us.

5. Job Lived a Life of Personal Righteousness

Everything I did was honest. Righteousness covered me like a robe, and I wore justice like a turban. I served as eyes for the blind and feet for the lame. I was a father to the poor and assisted strangers who needed help. I broke the jaws of godless oppressors and plucked their victims from their teeth.

(Job 29:14-17)

He pursued righteousness and it clothed him. His righteousness protected and preserved him. And the same should go for the Christians of today. So many of today's heroes appear to us as "good guys," but they are wolfs in sheep clothing. Beware, they will disappoint you! The only way to avoid this from happening is to be meticulous about holiness, in other words, pursue holiness on a daily basis. We need to put on righteousness.

And all who have been united with Christ in baptism have put on Christ, like putting on new clothes.

(Galatians 3:27)

91

> *Put on your new nature, and be renewed as you learn to know your Creator and become like him. In this new life, it doesn't matter if you are a Jew or a Gentile, circumcised or uncircumcised, barbaric, uncivilized, slave, or free. Christ is all that matters, and he lives in all of us. Since God chose you to be the holy people he loves, you must clothe yourselves with tenderhearted mercy, kindness, humility, gentleness, and patience.*

(Colossians 3:10-12)

We are not to give in to falsehood, deception, and or any form of impurity. Our minds should be filled with pure thoughts of God and our hearts will not be defiled. If we are to be protected, we have to pursue righteousness. And that is why Psalm 24:4-6 made it clear that:

> *Only those whose hands and hearts are pure, who do not worship idols and never tell lies. They will receive the Lord's blessing and have a right relationship with God their savior. Such people may seek you and worship in your presence, O God of Jacob.*

So also in Job 29:21-25, Job illustrates the extent of his wisdom thus:

6. Job Was a Well of Wisdom

> *Everyone listened to my advice. They were silent as they waited for me to speak. And after I spoke, they had nothing to add, for my counsel satisfied them. They longed for me to speak as people long for rain. They drank my words like a refreshing spring rain. When they were discouraged, I smiled at them. My look of approval was precious to them. Like a chief, I told them what to do.*

I lived like a king among his troops and comforted those who mourned.

Furthermore, the subject of wisdom can also be found in James 1:5. It states that: *If you need wisdom, ask our generous God, and he will give it to you. He will not rebuke you for asking.*

Job spoke and everyone listened. They knew whatever came out of Job's mouth was profitable! Job had true wisdom and insight, not political rhetoric borne of personal ambition or manipulation. True wisdom is born of God. You, like Job, can have that same kind of wisdom, and you should. We can ask God for it and He will give it liberally in the name of Jesus. It is not enough to quote scripture to the world, but we need to share the wisdom and the power of the Word with the people around us. And by doing so, we will become the light of the world as portrayed in Matthew 5:14: *You are the light of the world — like a city on a hilltop that cannot be hidden.*

And that means that whoever loves wisdom makes those around him rejoice. Wisdom gives life. Wisdom gives strength. And wisdom gives a good defense because it comes from God. The loss of manhood in America today is embedded in the fact that, men have lost the desire for this great pearl. In other words the kingdom of God is compared to an awesome pearl as Matthew 13:45-46 rightly emphasize that: *Again, the Kingdom of Heaven is like a merchant on the lookout for choice pearls. When he discovered a pearl of great value, he sold everything he owned and bought it!*

We as today's Christians need to go all out to obtain this precious pearl.

7. Job was a Pursuer of God

Job was first and foremost a pursuer of God. Pursuit of God is a mark of a real man. That may sound foreign to us because we live in a culture where religion has, for years, been the domain of women. Men have been programmed to believe that being a real man and serving God somehow does not go together. But Job shows us differently. All the character traits that we have seen in Job were made possible because of his relationship with God. It was because of God's mercy that Job was merciful. And in Lamentations 3:22, the word of God states that: *The faithful love of the Lord never ends! His mercies never cease.*

> *God blesses those who are merciful, for they will be shown mercy.*
>
> **(Matthew 5:7)**

It was because God is just that Job sought justice. It was because God hates evil that Job broke the jaws of the wicked. His life, in all his masculine expression, was built around his worship of God. Apparently his pursuit of God molded him into the kind of man he was. That is why God approved Job as a model for true manhood.

These are part of the reasons why God referred to Job thus: *Then the Lord asked Satan, "Have you noticed my servant Job? He is the finest man in all the earth. He is blameless – a man of complete integrity. He fears God and stays away from evil"* (Job 1:8).

Job was a Real Man, real hero and a model for all men to follow and imitate. Keep striving for excellence, one day, God will boast of you to demons and principalities in the name of Jesus.

Chapter Ten

The Spiritually Mature Man

⮰

Children are lovely gifts and Psalm 127:5 states: *How joyful is the man whose quiver is full of them! He will not be put to shame when he confronts his accusers at the city gates.*

You ought to have as many as you wish! They are delightful and it is an enjoyable experience to watch them grow up to become men and women. However, you and I know that there are some things about little babies that are not very attractive (we humor them because they are babies).

Those things that are part of babyhood include the following:

- They are dependent and demanding
- They are unable to feed themselves
- They are unable to stay out of messes
- They love to be the center of attention
- They are driven by impulses, such as hunger, pain, sleep
- They are irritated when they are dirty (*even though they make the mess and you have to clean them*)

- They have no manners, no control
- They have little attention span, no concern for others, no abilities or skills.

When you see adults with those characteristics, something tragic has happened, something terribly unfunny. The Christian, who is not interested in growing up, wants to be entertained. Whenever you see Christians fussing, quarrelling about their own rights, complaining because they are not properly recognized, and whining that they do not get enough applause of what they do – "baby spirit" is indicated.

What is Maturity?

One of Webster's definitions says that maturity is "a state being perfect, complete or ready." Maturity is the ability to do a job whether supervised or not; finish it once started; carry money without spending it and bear an injustice without getting even. It is the ability to disagree without being disagreeable.

In the real sense of it, a mature adult is self-reliant and able to take care of himself. He has the ability to help others. He has reached a state of physical and mental ripening. He is able to reason, decide, and act with a degree of wisdom. The plan and the purpose of God for us is to mature (grow up) so that we are spiritually perfect, complete and ready. How dangerous or wrong is it to be spiritually immature?

> *But people who **aren't spiritual** can't receive these truths from God's Spirit. It all sounds foolish to them*

*and they can't understand it, for only those **who are spiritual** can understand what the Spirit means.*

(1 Corinthians 2:14)

Dear brothers and sisters, when I was with you I couldn't talk to you as I would to spiritual people. I had to talk as though you belonged to this world or as though you were infants in the Christian life. I had to feed you with milk, not with solid food, because you weren't ready for anything stronger. And you still aren't ready, for you are still controlled by your sinful nature. You are jealous of one another and quarrel with each other. Doesn't that prove you are controlled by your sinful nature? Aren't you living like people of the world?

(1 Corinthians 3:1-3)

There are two kinds of people: *Natural* people, who are unsaved (1 Corinthians 2:14), and *Spiritual* people, who were sinners, but are justified by God's grace through the redemption in Christ Jesus (Romans 3:23-24). Out of the people who are saved, are *Carnal* people, who have one foot in Christ and the other in the world. They have a salvation experience but are immature, allowing their fleshly nature to control them. They are "brethren," but are "babes in Christ" (1 Corinthians 3:1), because they *lack spiritual growth* (1 Corinthians 3:2).

The contrast between a carnal man and a spiritual man, and between carnal mindedness and spiritual mindedness, is very strongly expressed by Apostle Paul in Romans 8:5, 6:

Those who are dominated by the sinful nature think about sinful things, but those who are controlled by the

Holy Spirit think about things that please the Spirit. So letting your sinful nature control your mind leads to death. But letting the Spirit control your mind leads to life and peace.

You have been believers so long now that you ought to be teaching others. Instead, you need someone to teach you again the basic things about God's word. You are like babies who need milk and cannot eat solid food. For someone who lives on milk is still an infant and doesn't know how to do what is right. Solid food is for those who are mature, who through training have the skill to recognize the difference between right and wrong. And who then turn away from God. It is impossible to bring such people back to repentance; by rejecting the Son of God, they themselves are nailing him to the cross once again and holding him up to public shame.

Let us stop going over the basic teachings about Christ again and again. Let us go on instead and become mature in our understanding. Surely we don't need to start again with the fundamental importance of repenting from evil deeds and placing our faith in God. You don't need further instruction about baptisms, the laying on of hands, the resurrection of the dead, and eternal judgment. And so, God willing, we will move forward to further understanding. For it is impossible to bring back to repentance those who were once enlightened – those who have experienced the good things of heaven and shared in the Holy Spirit, who have tasted the goodness of the word of God and the power of the age to come – and who then turn away from God. It is impossible to bring such people back to repentance; by rejecting the Son of God, they themselves are nailing him to the cross once again and holding him up to public shame.

(Hebrews 6:1-6)

Stages of Maturity

The four essential stages of maturity namely: *Help Me; Tell Me; Show Me and Follow Me* are explained below.

1. Help Me - Infancy Stage

Newborn babies are frail, dependent, and completely incapable of discerning danger. The indiscriminating infant Christians will often grab for appealing false teaching, not realizing the risk. Believers in this stage cry out, "Help me!" Just surviving is their main focus. Until they begin to walk on their own, more mature Christians must spoon-feed them with God's Word and give them constant attention. For example, in Romans 7:7-25, the word of God elaborates more clearly how Christians especially those at the infancy stage could stay away from sin of any type if they are really ready to grow into mature Christians.

Well then, am I suggesting that the law of God is sinful? Of course not! In fact, it was the law that showed me my sin. I would never have known that coveting is wrong if the law had not said, "You must not covet." [8] But sin used this command to arouse all kinds of covetous desires within me! If there were no law, sin would not have that power. [9] At one time I lived without understanding the law. But when I learned the command not to covet, for instance, the power of sin came to life, [10] and I died. So I

99

discovered that the law's commands, which were supposed to bring life, brought spiritual death instead. ¹¹ Sin took advantage of those commands and deceived me; it used the commands to kill me. ¹² But still, the law itself is holy, and its commands are holy and right and good. ¹³But how can that be? Did the law, which is good, cause my death? Of course not! Sin used what was good to bring about my condemnation to death. So we can see how terrible sin really is. It uses God's good commands for its own evil purposes. ¹⁴ So the trouble is not with the law, for it is spiritual and good. The trouble is with me, for I am all too human, a slave to sin. ¹⁵ I don't really understand myself, for I want to do what is right, but I don't do it. Instead, I do what I hate. ¹⁶ But if I know that what I am doing is wrong, this shows that I agree that the law is good. ¹⁷ So I am not the one doing wrong; it is sin living in me that does it.

It continues from chapter 18 thus:

And I know that nothing good lives in me, that is, in my sinful nature. I want to do what is right, but I can't. ¹⁹ I want to do what is good, but I don't. I don't want to do what is wrong, but I do it anyway. ²⁰ But if I do what I don't want to do, I am not really the one doing wrong; it is sin living in me that does it. ²¹ I have discovered this principle of life – that when I want to do what is right, I inevitably do what is wrong. ²² I love God's law with all my heart. ²³ But there is another power[c] within me that is at war with my mind. This power makes me a slave to the sin that is still within me. ²⁴ Oh, what a miserable person I am! Who will free me from this life that is dominated by sin and death? ²⁵ Thank God! The *answer is in Jesus Christ our Lord. So you see how it is: In my mind I really want to obey God's law, but because of my sinful nature I am a slave to sin.*

(Romans 7:7-25)

The mark of a maturing Christian is that he continues to walk the walk, not just talk the talk. Many who portray themselves as Christians pretend but have little or no substance according to the criteria found in the Bible.

Paul said in Colossians 1:28 that his purpose for preaching the gospel was *We want to present them to God, perfect in their relationship to Christ.*

The word translated "perfect" means complete, mature, or full grown. It does not mean flawless. Paul knew that it is not enough just to preach the first principles, but we must go on to perfection.

Yet when I am among mature believers, I do speak with words of wisdom, but not the kind of wisdom that belongs to this world or to the rulers of this world, who are soon forgotten.
(1 Corinthians 2:6)

So let us stop going over the basic teachings about Christ again and again. Let us go on instead and become mature in our understanding. Surely we don't need to start again with the fundamental importance of repenting from evil deeds and placing our faith in God.
(Hebrews 6:1)

All Christians need to be mature, self-reliant, and able to help others spiritually. We must desire the sincere (pure) milk of the word that we may grow to maturity as the word of God shows in 1 Peter 2:2: *Like newborn babies, you must crave pure spiritual milk so that you will grow into a full experience of salvation.* Cry out for this nourishment.

The Struggle Against Sin

Too many of us men exhibit behaviors that do not reflect what God expects of a man. These vices violate biblical principles.

Paul wrote to the Romans:

> *I don't really understand myself, for I want to do what is right, but I don't do it. Instead, I do what I hate.*
>
> **(Romans 7:15)**

> *But there is another power within me that is at war with my mind. This power makes me a slave to the sin that is still within me. ²⁴ Oh, what a miserable person I am! Who will free me from this life that is dominated by sin and death? ²⁵ Thank God! The answer is in Jesus Christ our Lord. So you see how it is: In my mind I really want to obey God's law, but because of my sinful nature I am a slave to sin.*
>
> **(Romans 7:23-25)**

Listed below are several forms of extreme behavior that men fall into, which do not glorify God.

Playboy: This is a man who pursues a life of pleasure without responsibility, and also lacks sexual self-control. His sexual appetite controls his life like King Solomon as portrayed in 1 Kings 11:1-3 thus:

Now King Solomon loved many foreign women. Besides Pharaoh's daughter, he married women from Moab, Ammon, Edom, Sidon, and from among the Hittites. ² The Lord had clearly instructed the people of Israel, 'You must not marry them, because they will turn your hearts to their gods.' Yet Solomon insisted on loving them anyway. ³ He had 700 wives of royal birth and 300 concubines. And in fact, they did turn his heart away from the Lord.

Macho Man: Here is a man who is characterized by qualities considered manly, especially when manifested in an assertive, self-conscious, or dominating way. This man believes that to be masculine is to show off muscles and be a mastery of women. A good example of this is Samson who lost his strength in Judges 16:1-3:

One day Samson went to the Philistine town of Gaza and spent the night with a prostitute. ² Word soon spread that Samson was there, so the men of Gaza gathered together and waited all night at the town gates. They kept quiet during the night, saying to themselves, "When the light of morning comes, we will kill him." But Samson stayed in bed only until midnight. Then he got up, took hold of the doors of the town gate, including the two posts, and lifted them up, bar and all. He put them on his shoulders and carried them all the way to the top of the hill across from Hebron.

(Judges 16:1-3)

Mama's Boy: This is an adult male who has never cut his mother's apron strings. Thus, his mother still controls his life. Jacob is an example of this.

103

> *Rebekah said to her son Jacob, "Look, I overheard your*
> *father say to your brother Esau, ⁷ 'Bring me some game*
> *and prepare me some tasty food to eat, so that I may*
> *give you my blessing in the presence of the L*ord *before*
> *I die.'"*
>
> **(Genesis 27:6-7)**

Tinkerer: This is a person who busies himself with various kinds of work without useful results; jack-of-all-trades. He is the kind of person who is preoccupied with his hobby than he does with people like Jehu in 2 Kings 10:16. *Then Jehu said, "Now come with me, and see how devoted I am to the Lord." So Jehonadab rode along with him.*

Jellyfish: This category of man allows his friends, wife, children and co-workers to walk all over him. More of this behavior can be found in Judges 11:2: *Gilead's wife also had several sons, and when these half brothers grew up, they chased Jephthah off the land. "You will not get any of our father's inheritance," they said, "for you are the son of a prostitute."*

General: This is the kind of man who is a boss, husband, church officer, or community leader, and he who barks orders like Cornelius.

> *In Caesarea there lived a Roman army officer named*
> *Cornelius, who was a captain of the Italian Regiment.*
> *² He was a devout, God-fearing man, as was everyone in*
> *his household. He gave generously to the poor and prayed*
> *regularly to God.*
>
> **(Acts 10:1-2)**

Gym Rat: This man's thought and energies go into watching and participating in sports. Nimrod was a man in these shoes.

Since he was the greatest hunter in the world, his name became proverbial. People would say, "This man is like Nimrod, the greatest hunter in the world."

(Genesis 10:9)

Gay Guy: This kind of man may have male bodily figure, but his mind and actions contradict his sexual identity.

That is why God abandoned them to their shameful desires. Even the women turned against the natural way to have sex and instead indulged in sex with each other.

(Romans 1:26)

Workaholic: Here is a man who regards his job as his first responsibility, his source of satisfaction and security like Esau in **Genesis 27:30-31:**

As soon as Isaac had finished blessing Jacob, and almost before Jacob had left his father, Esau returned from his hunt. 31 Esau prepared a delicious meal and brought it to his father. Then he said, "Sit up, my father, and eat my wild game so you can give me your blessing."

Zombie: This man grew up thinking that a man should never have emotions – so he does not have. An example was Joab, nephew of King David and the commander of his army.

There he proclaimed Ishbosheth king over Gilead, Jezreel, Ephraim, Benjamin, the land of the Ashurites, and all the rest of Israel. Ishbosheth, Saul's son, was forty years old when he became king, and he ruled from Mahanaim for two years. Meanwhile, the people of

Judah remained loyal to David. David made Hebron his capital, and he ruled as king of Judah for seven and a half years.

(2 Samuel. 2:9-11)

2. Tell Me - Childhood Stage
(Servants in the Kingdom of God)

In the second stage of maturity, the focus is learning. Believers in this phase are just beginning to feed themselves God's truths, and their joy of discovery is thrilling. "Tell me!" is their cry, and their enthusiasm and curiosity seem boundless. The danger, however, is that their discernment is limited. Easily persuaded, they can be tempted to follow any strong authority figure. This stage eventually ends when they are able to reproduce their faith in others.

What is your potential in the Kingdom of God? He has called you to be servants to minister to His church. The illustration of a young man is instructive at this juncture: He saw a military recruiting commercial on television. He observed a classy naval man near his age dressed in a sharp uniform on the deck of a remarkable ship sailing the open seas with beautiful crystal sky, smiling with his mates.

The commercial then showed this sailor in ports all over the world, and it's all free. He went for the gimmick and signed up. However, at basic training, he could not sleep when he wanted, ordered to cut his hair, he could not go to many social gatherings and he got on a regimented schedule. All the while, he was cleaning bathrooms and messy halls and doing pushups and other difficult exercises. Later on, he was offended, felt cheated; in his eyes, he was sold a package that showed him only the benefits but didn't know the personal cost.

In Colossians 1:23-29, God word states that:

> But you must continue to believe this truth and stand firmly in it. Don't drift away from the assurance you received when you heard the Good News. The Good News has been preached all over the world, and I, Paul, have been appointed as God's servant to proclaim it. [24]I am glad when I suffer for you in my body, for I am participating in the sufferings of Christ that continue for his body, the church. [25] God has given me the responsibility of serving his church by proclaiming his entire message to you. [26]This message was kept secret for centuries and generations past, but now it has been revealed to God's people. [27]For God wanted them to know that the riches and glory of Christ are for you Gentiles, too. And this is the secret: Christ lives in you. This gives you assurance of sharing his glory. [28]So we tell others about Christ, warning everyone and teaching everyone with all the wisdom God has given us. We want to present them to God, perfect in their relationship to Christ. [29]That's why I work and struggle so hard, depending on Christ's mighty power that works within me.

And Psalm 18:20 states that:

> The Lord rewarded me for doing right; he restored me because of my innocence.

For we are both God's workers. And you are God's field.
You are God's building.[10] *Because of God's grace to me,*
I have laid the foundation like an expert builder. Now
others are building on it. But whoever is building on this
foundation must be very careful.[11] *For no one can lay any*
foundation other than the one we already have – Jesus
Christ.[12] *Anyone who builds on that foundation may*
use a variety of materials – gold, silver, jewels, wood,
hay, or straw.[13] *But on the judgment day, fire will reveal*
what kind of work each builder has done. The fire will
show if a person's work has any value.[14] *If the work*
survives, that builder will receive a reward.[15] *But if the*
work is burned up, the builder will suffer great loss. The
builder will be saved, but like someone barely escaping
through a wall of flames.[16] *Don't you realize that all of*
you together are the temple of God and that the Spirit
of God lives in you?[17] *God will destroy anyone who*
destroys this temple. For God's temple is holy, and you
are that temple.

(1 Corinthians 3:9-17)

Servants are actually set-ups for miracles. They are either beneficiaries of miracles or instrumental to their occurrence. Those who are ready to serve are really ready for breakthroughs. The *Widow of Zarephath* and *Simon the Fisherman* were great examples of service unto testimonies. It is also worthy of note that a servant girl was instrumental to Naaman's healing (2 Kings 5). Elisha was the servant of Elijah (And also the servant of God).

Gehazi was the servant of Elisha. Naaman was the servant of the king of Syria. The men who pacify the fury of Naaman at the doorstep of Elisha were the servants of Naaman. In Romans 1:1, Paul declared himself thus: *"Paul a bondservant of Christ Jesus called as an apostle."* Paul knew what he was called to be. Do you know your calling?

3. Show Me - Adolescence Stage
(Continual Testing period)

Believers passing through this phase are capable of reproducing their faith but are sometimes reluctant to do so. Their level of discernment is not always reliable, and they are often critical of others, yet unwilling to contribute anything themselves. They focus on challenging others, saying "Show me!" or "Prove it to me!" They don't settle for answers and the way things have always been; instead, they challenge others to rethink their beliefs and prove the integrity of their lives. They are often idealistic and intolerant. When they eventually shift their focus to the needs of others, they are ready to enter the next level.

Sometimes when a believer has been at a particular level of spiritual development for a long time, some tribulation may be necessary to "kick" the believer into the next phase of his or her walk with God.

In actuality, we are all being tested by fire. If we find that our faith is being eroded, each time trials or troubles comes along, perhaps we are like weak servants, who are not building with gold or silver or precious stones.

However, it is important to realize that God never abandons those who are His. After all, Romans 8:35 states that:

> *Can anything ever separate us from Christ's love? Does it mean he no longer loves us if we have trouble or*

calamity, or are persecuted, or hungry, or destitute, or in danger, or threatened with death? ³⁶ (As the Scriptures say, "For your sake we are killed every day; we are being slaughtered like sheep." ³⁷ No, despite all these things, overwhelming victory is ours through Christ, who loved us. ³⁸ And I am convinced that nothing can ever separate us from God's love. Neither death nor life, neither angels nor demons, neither our fears for today nor our worries about tomorrow – not even the powers of hell can separate us from God's love. ³⁹ No power in the sky above or in the earth below – indeed, nothing in all creation will ever be able to separate us from the love of God that is revealed in Christ Jesus our Lord.

(Romans 8:35-39)

4. Follow Me – Adulthood (Press On to Maturity)

This is a period of stability and balance. Adult Christians can easily spot a spiritual fraud because they have developed great discernment (Hebrews 5:14). With their focus on serving others, their cry is "Follow Me" as they follow Christ. They don't grasp at every Christian trend that breezes by. They know maturity is a lengthy process that requires "long obedience in the same directions."

Hebrews 6 lists seven doctrines of the Church of God and admonishes us to press on to maturity.

*So let us stop going over the basic teachings about Christ again and again. Let us **go on** instead and **become mature** in our understanding. Surely we don't need to start again with the fundamental importance of **repenting** from evil deeds and **placing our faith in God**. ² You don't need further instruction about baptisms, the **laying***

on of hands, the resurrection of the dead, and eternal judgment.

(Hebrews 6:1-2, NASB)

It was lack of maturity that plagued the church in Sardis (Revelations 3:1-6). The rewards mentioned in Revelation 3:4-5 should induce us to overcome the sins that ensnare us. God made the same offer to the church in Laodicea (Revelations 3:14-20). Here again, God encourages people to **do** things His way and be saved from eternal destruction – or to continue on as they are and be lost.

Perhaps the correct degree of maturity can best be described by **1 Corinthians 14:20, NASB**: *[be grown up]. Dear brothers and sisters don't be childish in your understanding of these things. Be innocent as babies when it comes to evil, but* **be mature** *in understanding matters of this kind.*

Chapter Eleven

The Carnal Man
vs.
The Spiritual Man

⌒

The seventh chapter of the book of Romans focused on gloom and condemnation, while the eighth chapter centered on glory and emancipation. The seventh chapter is a funeral march; the eighth is a wedding march. It's the song of a "soul set free," to use the phrase of a lovely hymn. Romans chapter seven is a chapter on the tomb but Romans chapter eight is a chapter on triumph.

To borrow John Milton's phrase, the Romans chapter seven is the chapter of paradise lost. It is a chapter of depravity, whereas the eighth is a chapter of deliverance and delight.

Chapter seven is a chapter of misery, whereas the eighth is a liberated soul. Also interestingly, the seventh is a chapter on a self-centered person but the eighth is about the Christ-centered person.

In the seventh chapter, the first person was mentioned over and over and over until it becomes too repetitive

"I, I, I," "I want to do this but I can't...," and "I find I am in bondage...," and so forth and so on. The "I"'s was mentioned about 41 times, and there was no mention of the Holy Spirit. In the eighth chapter there is no mention of the "I" except in two verses where it was stated "I reckon" and "I am persuaded" (where there is no alternative).

Chapter eight was different because the Holy Spirit was mentioned 19 times. Also, the chapter begins with, "there is no condemnation." And it ends with "there is no separation." In fact, it marks tribulation out for us very carefully, focuses on the liberated man, and pays tribute to the Holy Spirit of God.

Paul was talking about emancipation, how an individual having under his feet, the world, the flesh, and the devil. The devil! The devil never pushed the Apostle around, but he pushed the devil around! Probably when Paul died, they had a half-day's holiday in hell because he caused a major havoc on their territory and they were so glad he left. Paul was able to accomplish a great deal because he was energized and so drunk with the Holy Spirit.

That was why he said in **1 Corinthians 14:18** that:

I thank God that I speak in tongues more than any of you.

Paul, a man of purpose was not afraid to face challenges because he knew who he was in Christ Jesus. He was warned a few times of impending dangers, but did not heed the warning. He was more concerned how he would fulfill the will of God. Acts 21:10-14 illustrates this example thus:

Several days later a man named Agabus, who also had the gift of prophecy, arrived from Judea. ¹¹He came over, took Paul's belt, and bound his own feet and hands with it. Then he said, "The Holy Spirit declares, 'So shall the owner of this belt be bound by the Jewish leaders in Jerusalem and turned over to the Gentiles.'" ¹²When we heard this, we and the local believers all begged Paul not to go on to Jerusalem. ¹³But he said, "Why all this weeping? You are breaking my heart! I am ready not only to be jailed at Jerusalem but even to die for the sake of the Lord Jesus." ¹⁴When it was clear that we couldn't persuade him, we gave up and said, "The Lord's will be done."

(Acts 21:10-14, KJV)

Paul was not perturbed how terrible the malady was. He's concerned about the remedy! He had the revelation that we are equipped to overcome any challenges. That is why he said that. *No, despite all these things, overwhelming victory is ours through Christ, who loved us* (Romans 8:37). Dr. Tozer once said, "as soon as man got *alienated from God,* he got interested *in things.*" Now I was reading through these chapters, and I noticed how many times Paul says that, "They that are after the flesh do mind the *things* of the flesh, but they that are after the Spirit mind the *things* of the Spirit."

The man of chapter seven is born again, but lived in the flesh – Carnal man. A schizophrenic (skit-zo-phrenic) Christian is lovable when under the anointing, everyone wants to hug him or her. When he is not under the influence of the anointing however, he is angry and wimpy. He may be very big outwardly but hollow and feeble inside. However, the man of chapter 8 has the very spirit of God, that Jesus called "The Promise of the Father" – keep his flesh under, his soul is in tune with God, and he is obedient to the high call of God on his life. The analogy is like comparing Joseph with Samson.

The Pauline epistle to the Ephesians says that for believers to come to full maturity in Christ, they should grow beyond being just spiritual babes (Ephesians 4:11-16). Believers have to be rooted in God's Word so that they are not influenced by every doctrine that is communicated to them through television, friends, relatives, pamphlets, books, and mediums.

Remember the Bible states in **John 2:4-6** that:

> *If someone claims, "I know God," but doesn't obey God's commandments, that person is a liar and is not living in the truth.* *⁵ But those who obey God's word truly show how completely they love him. That is how we know we are living in him.* *⁶ Those who say they live in God should live their lives as Jesus did.*

Beware of television preachers who watered down God's Word! Anyone who continually feed on milk of the Word is obviously inexperienced in the doctrine of righteousness, for he is a mere infant. It is imperative to change our diet from milk to meat of the Word in order to become full-grown men. This will train our senses and mental faculties so that we would be able to discern both good and evil (Hebrews 5:14).

Comparison between Samson and Joseph

Joseph and Samson started their lives in very much the same way – both were anointed of God. Comparing these two vessels, it is very apparent Samson was not a good steward of the grace of God upon his life, but Joseph stayed through to the end, irrespective of what he was subjected to.

(i)   Joseph *(Genesis 37-39)*

Joseph went through different phases before he arrived at the final destination. His life story is quite revealing and the following points are to be noted:

- Joseph was raised by his father as a favorite son to be a good Israelite and the Lord talked with him in dreams. His brothers were jealous of him and eventually, he was sold into slavery in a foreign land.

  His brothers responded, "So you think you will be our king, do you? Do you actually think you will reign over us?" And they hated him all the more because of his dreams and the way he talked about them.

  (Genesis 37:8)

- Potiphar made Joseph the overseer of his house, and God blessed the Egyptian for Joseph's sake. **Genesis 39:6** reads thus:

  So Potiphar gave Joseph complete administrative responsibility over everything he owned. With Joseph there, he didn't worry about a thing – except what kind of food to eat! Joseph was a very handsome and well-built young man.

117

• Joseph could be angry, saying, "What's the use of keeping the laws of the God of my father? He's done nothing for me because my own brothers sold me into slavery!" If you develop your inner man (the anointing within) as strong as the anointing upon you, your life will be a good example to others. Like Joseph, you will be well favored. But if your human spirit becomes weaker as the days go by, then your life can become more bizarre. The fact that Joseph refused Potiphar's wife, when asked to sleep with her (Genesis 39:7-9), is an indication that he has a strong inner man. The physical body wants sex, rest and play. It does not recognize covenants. It does not see the wedding ring – it only wants to satisfy its desire. Your body has no conscience – it just has wants.

• Here is a young man who was enslaved in a foreign country, yet, kept to the covenant of his God. He had something built up on the inside that gave him the ability to realize God had control of his life, distance notwithstanding. His spiritual stamina strengthened him to say "NO" to Potiphar's wife! He knew that this act will not only violate his covenant with his master, but will also defy a greater one with his God.

• Joseph did what was right. He kept to the law of his God and did not let the trauma of his soul or the enticement of his flesh pulled him to sin. He was mature to hold the reins of his being. *You can get there too!*

(ii)   Samson (Judges 16)

Samson was another anointed vessel of God, a paragon of power, but how far did he go?

- Samson had a magnificent life from the start. An angel appeared to his mother and told her not to eat or drink any unclean thing while she was pregnant. The Holy Spirit came on him when he was a child – *Wow!*

- His problems started when he refused to marry a girl among the tribes of Israel. Instead, he chose a Philistine woman to be his wife. He married outside the will of God. To further buttress this assertion, In Judges 16:1, the Bible states: *One day Samson went to the Philistine town of Gaza and spent the night with a prostitute.* All that happened in one verse. He was not like Joseph. At least Joseph was tempted several times before he finally refused his boss' wife. Samson gave in to just one temptation.

  Read **Judges 16:2-6**: *...Word soon spread that Samson was there, so the men of Gaza gathered together and waited all night at the town gates. They kept quiet during the night, saying to themselves, "When the light of morning comes, we will kill him." So Delilah said to Samson, "Please tell me what makes you so strong and what it would take to tie you up securely."*

Samson loved Delilah so much that he succumbed to her pressure of wanting to know the secrets of his power.

- Samson was not taken captive rather he was out playing with his destiny. He had the greater anointing which was more or less raw anointing and strength, but when he went down to Gaza, fell in love with a woman who tricked him. Three times Samson mocked and told Delilah lies (Judges 16:10, 16-17). The first time she asked, *"tell me where your strength is,"* [...] *So Delilah said to Samson, "Please tell me what makes you so strong and what it would take to tie you up securely."* He should have stormed out of the house and made a hole in the wall on his way out. But foolishly, he kept entertaining her requests. Even though, he was heavily anointed, he was weak inside. Anointing does not resist the devil and does not stop temptation. You have to develop your inner man to successfully oppose the devil.

- If everything depended on the anointing, then Samson won't have fallen to the traps of Satan, and more so, Delilah would have been dead. But the story went on until she discovered the secret of his strength that eventually led to his downfall.

Then she cried out, "Samson! The Philistines have come to capture you!" When he woke up, he thought, "I will do as before and shake myself free." But he didn't realize the Lord had left him.²¹ So the Philistines captured him and gouged out his eyes. They took him to Gaza, where he was bound with bronze chains and forced to grind grain in the prison.

(Judges 16:20-21)

Beloved, if you do not build a strong spirit like Joseph, you will lose the ability to see and discern. This negligence could cost you your liberty because you might end up exerting energy in another man's labor. God forbid that concerning you in the name of Jesus.

Marks of Maturity

Spiritual maturity doesn't happen overnight. When John wrote his first epistle, he mentioned little children, children, young men and fathers **(1 John 2:12-14)** – each at a different level of growth.

> *I am writing to you who are God's children because your sins have been forgiven through Jesus.*[13] *I am writing to you who are mature in the faith because you know Christ, who existed from the beginning. I am writing to you who are young in the faith because you have won your battle with the evil one.* [14] *I have written to you who are God's children because you know the Father. I have written to you who are mature in the faith because you know Christ, who existed from the beginning. I have written to you who are young in the faith because you are strong. God's word lives in your hearts, and you have won your battle with the evil one.*

Although, it's not always easy to pinpoint a person's maturity level; the following nine marks of Spiritual Maturity will help to measure your maturity:

1. Spiritual people based their lives and decisions on their personal relationship with God, Christ, and His Word. For example 1 Corinthians 2:14, 16 explains this assertion thus: *But people who aren't spiritual can't receive these truths from God's Spirit. It all sounds foolish to them and they can't understand it, for only those who are spiritual can*

understand what the Spirit means. You have been believers so long now that you ought to be teaching others. Instead, you need someone to teach you again the basic things about God's word. You are like babies who need milk and cannot eat solid food. [13] For someone who lives on milk is still an infant and doesn't know how to do what is right. [14] Solid food is for those who are mature, who through training have the skill to recognize the difference between right and wrong. 6 So let us stop going over the basic teachings about Christ again and again. Let us go on instead and become mature in our understanding. Surely we don't need to start again with the fundamental importance of repenting from evil deeds and placing our faith in God. [2] You don't need further instruction about baptisms, the laying on of hands, the resurrection of the dead, and eternal judgment. [3] And so, God willing, we will move forward to further understanding. [4] For it is impossible to bring back to repentance those who were once enlightened – those who have experienced the good things of heaven and shared in the Holy Spirit, [5] who have tasted the goodness of the word of God and the power of the age to come – [6] and who then turn away from God. It is impossible to bring such people back to repentance; by rejecting the Son of God, they themselves are nailing him to the cross once again and holding him up to public shame.

(Hebrews 5:12 - 6:6, NASB)

2.   A mature believer is one who no longer stumbles over his tongue. James draws our attention to one thing: the use of the tongue. He makes it the acid test of spiritual maturity. He writes; *…Indeed, we all make many mistakes. For if we could control our tongues, we would be perfect and could also control ourselves in every other way.*

(James 3:2)

A spiritually mature person controls his tongue. If a man cannot control his tongue, he is not spiritually mature. You may say "Oh, but he prays such wonderful prayers." But does it really matter? The fact that "He's a leader in the church" is not a criterion. The reason being that "He's a loving, generous person" is not the issue. The real test of maturity is whether he can control his tongue or not.

Apostle James is not talking about simply *"Christianizing"* – my vocabulary. He is telling us to examine our speaking habits. Do our words hurt, or do they heal? Do they inspire, or do they hurt? Do we seem harsh and unloving, or compassionate and caring? Does pressure make us unkind and irritable, or is the fruit of the spirit still evident in our lives?

3. Mature believers do not nurse un-confessed sins. They refuse to feed their old nature and starve their new nature. This amounts to the real cause of division in the Body of Christ. Do not walk as carnal men, but be spiritual and walk in the spirit as it is portrayed in 1 Corinthians 13:3-4, according to NASB:

    If I gave everything I have to the poor and even sacrificed my body, I could boast about it; but if I didn't love others, I would have gained nothing.⁴ Love is patient and kind. Love is not jealous or boastful or proud.

4. Mature believers do not adopt a self-righteous attitude toward others with a Talmud of *"thou shalts"* and *"thou shalt nots"*. They use their gifts to build instead of boasting (1 Corinthians. 13:4).

5. A mature church grows in Unity **(1 Corinthians 3:5-9a).** It is not the planters or the *waterers* that get the glory, but God who gives the increase. Mature believers serve the Church by showing acts of love and concern toward everyone. Love includes patience and understanding.

    After all, who is Apollos? Who is Paul? We are only God's servants through whom you believed the Good News. Each of us did the work the Lord gave us. [6] I planted the seed in your hearts, and Apollos watered it, but it was God who made it grow. [7] It's not important who does the planting, or who does the watering. What's important is that God makes the seed grow. [8] The one who plants and the one who waters work together with the same purpose. And both will be rewarded for their own hard work. [9] For we are both God's workers. And you are God's field. You are God's building.

6. The mature Christian sees to it that not only are buildings on the right foundation, but that proper materials based on God's Word are used. Many standards (modern, My, Revised, Traditional) and all such phenomena are not God's standards. In 1 Corinthians 3:9-15, according to NASB, the word of God states that:

    For we are both God's workers. And you are God's field. You are God's building. [10] Because of God's grace to me, I have laid the foundation like an expert builder. Now others are building on it. But whoever is building on this foundation must be very careful. [11] For no one can lay any foundation other than the one we already have – Jesus Christ. [12] Anyone who builds on that foundation may use a variety of materials – gold, silver, jewels, wood, hay, or straw. ¹³ *But on the judgment day, fire will reveal what kind of work each builder has done. The fire will show if a person's work has any value.* ¹⁴ *If the work survives, that builder will receive a reward.* ¹⁵ *But if the work is burned up, the builder will suffer great loss. The builder will be saved, but like someone barely escaping through a wall of flames.*

Isaiah 28:16 (KJV) says:

Therefore, this is what the Sovereign Lord says: "Look! I am placing a foundation stone in Jerusalem, a firm and tested stone. It is a precious cornerstone that is safe to build on. Whoever believes need never be shaken."

7. The mature are aware that at the judgment seat of Christ, all works will be revealed – not quantity, but the quality (1 Corinthians 3:15). Christians ought not to be evaluating life solely on the present or visible conditions.

    If it is burned up, the builder will suffer loss but yet will be saved – even though only as one escaping through the flames.
    (1 Corinthians 3:15, NASB)

8. Purity is taught and lived. We are God's temple that MUST be kept pure. In Jewish custom, the temple is *corrupted* or *destroyed* when anyone defiled or in the slightest degree damaged anything in it, or if its guardians neglected their duties. And in 1 Corinthians 3:16-17, according to NASB, the Word of God states:

125

> *Don't you realize that all of you together are the temple
> of God and that the Spirit of God lives in you? God
> will destroy anyone who destroys this temple. For God's
> temple is holy, and you are that temple.*

9. Mature Christians learn to discern between good and
    evil, and conduct themselves according to the Word of
    God. Believers must focus on God's Word, so that they
    will not be swayed by the evil and deceptive influences
    of the society. If our surroundings contradict or
    violate our Christian values, separate yourself from
    those surroundings. It should be *spiritually natural* for
    Christians to run from hazards. This is portrayed in
    Proverbs 5:8-9, ASV thus: *Remove thy way far from her,
    And come not nigh the door of her house; [9]Lest thou give thine
    honor unto others, And thy years unto the cruel.*

Spiritual people do not blame every problem on Satan.
Most problems come from us. A good example is depicted
in Proverbs 26:2, NASB: *Like a fluttering sparrow or a dart-
ing swallow, an undeserved curse will not land on its intended victim.* The above Scripture implies that some curses are de-
served i.e. caused by the victim. A mature person takes the
responsibility for his failures and makes needed changes.

Mature people stay humble, respect authority and keep
learning. They do not sever human relationships just because there is a conflict with our leaders or those in civil
authority.

Pray for leaders – Many seemingly good people will be
turned away at the gate. Be sure you are not one of them.
For example, in 1 Corinthians 3:18-20, according to NASB
version, the Bible states:

*Stop deceiving yourselves. If you think you are wise by this world's standards, you need to become a fool to be truly wise. ¹⁹For the wisdom of this world is foolishness to God. As the Scriptures say, "He **traps the wise in the snare of their own cleverness.** ²⁰And again, "The Lord knows the thoughts of the wise; he knows they are worthless."*

(Cross references: Job 5:12-13; Proverbs 94:11)

Exalting people perpetuates immaturity and leads to failure. 1 Corinthians 3:21-23 teaches us that our boasting should not be in men. We need to make good decisions by exercising wisdom. A multitude of counselors will help.

So don't boast about following a particular human leader. For everything belongs to you — ²² whether Paul or Apollos or Peter, or the world, or life and death, or the present and the future. Everything belongs to you, ²³ and you belong to Christ, and Christ belongs to God.

For example in 1 Corinthians 3:21-23, the Bible emphasizes that: *Where there is no counsel, the people fall; But in the multitude of counselors there is safety.* Furthermore, Proverbs 12:15 states that: *Fools think their own way is right, but the wise listen to others.*

In conclusion, a mature man in Christ is indifferent to praises or blames. Brethren, it is my prayer that God will deliver us from our *babyishness.* How do you use your tongue? Are you a Samson or a Joseph? Is your life reflecting Romans chapter 7 or Romans chapter 8? Brethren, let's walk the walk of Christian maturity.

God made babies to grow. Listen to the admonition of a 5 year old, "God made me a baby, I grow the rest myself." If babies do not grow, something is seriously wrong, and death is imminent. God made Christians to grow. If we do not grow, something is seriously wrong, and eternal spiritual death is imminent. Let us "grow in grace and in the knowledge of Our Lord and Savior Jesus Christ."

> *Rather, you must grow in the grace and knowledge of our Lord and Savior Jesus Christ. All glory to him, both now and forever! Amen.*
>
> **(2 Peter 3:18)**

Chapter Twelve
Created for Victory

◦⌒◦

There are certain questions that everyone must ask in order to determine whether his life will be victorious or not. Just like the life of Joseph as enumerated previously, or the life of Samson full of shame, failure and reproach as a result of sin and disobedience. Remember that children of God are created for victory and are meant to be men and women of valor. But when we allow sin to overwhelm us, then, it becomes possible to come crashing down like a pack of cards as it is depicted in the life of Samson. But it is my ultimate prayer that our life should be victorious like that of Joseph no matter what time and situation may bring.

Therefore, these five questions will have different answers because we all have different personalities, experiences, habits, make-ups and hearts. The totality of man is dependent on these questions, and even Jesus had to answer these questions in order to be a success story. These five questions of life will set one's life.

1. **Who am I?** (One's identity)

If you cannot answer the question of whom you are, then

people will define your identity. You will be at the mercy of others if you are unable to answer this question. If you can be defined by others, you can be manipulated. In Acts 19:13-16, the sons of Sceva were defeated because they did not know their identity. Without knowing your identity, life is meaningless (Genesis 17:1).

2. **Where am I from?** (One's heritage or source)

The honor and respect that a man gets has a lot to do with where he is from – John 8:14, 1 Samuel 14:45.

3. **What am I sent here to do on earth?** (One's purpose)

Abuse is inevitable if the purpose of something is not understood. You are still alive because your purpose on earth is not yet fulfilled. Know that your life is not an accident. John 8:12, Jesus' purpose was to be light of the world. Luke 19:12. In 1 Corinthians 10:14, we see that God created marriage so that His name may be glorified. Jonah 9:3, Jonah's purpose was to go to Nineveh, when he did not fulfill his purpose, he went down. Acts 9:15, Paul's purpose was to bear the gospel to the Gentiles.

4. **What are my capabilities?** (One's potential)

Not knowing your potential makes you limited to what people can say you can do. David's potential was not realized by many people including his father and siblings. When Samuel was sent to choose a king, David was the least person on anyone's mind as the possible king. David, though, never doubted his potential. Commenting on Acts 13:22, Lloyd Jones says that "the men who tried to do something and fail are infinitely better than the men who do nothing and succeed." God gives you an opportunity to try again if you fail at something, so failure does not define your potential. In 1 Samuel 17:28-33, Saul's words to David were that he's not able to go against Goliath because he was just a youth and Goliath had been fighting since he was a youth. In verse 34-36, we see that David unlike others knew his potential. Know that any friend that does not encourage you to get to the next level and does not add to your life, you need to dump that person. Only failures make excuses.

5.   **Where am I going?** (One's destiny)

You will end up somewhere else if you do not know where you are going. John 8:14. 2 Timothy 4:6-7. A question to think about is that of will I finish well?

Knowing why you are in a place will remove any discouragement anyone may bring to make you leave. David's several victories are tied to him being able to answer these five questions above.

How Are the Mighty Men Falling?

David was a man of destiny and purpose, yet he fell. There are four questions that suggest how mighty men are falling.

1.   There is no place for **idleness** in the journey of life. There is a time for battle, and in the story of David, during the time of battle, he was sleeping. His idleness brought the opportunity for the enemy to find and finish him. He committed adultery with Bathsheba and that was the beginning of his downfall.

Idleness is dangerous. St. Augustine tells us: "Keep adding, keep walking, keep advancing, do not stop, do not turn back."

2. No place for **pride** in the battle of life. Proverbs 25:23, 1 Peter 5:5.

3. Your last victory is the greatest enemy of the last battle you are about to fight. The two hardest things to handle in life are **failure** and **success**.

4. The battle against **sin** is the fiercest battle you can ever fight.

Pray for holiness on a daily basis. Like Heavy man Jim said: "Fight one more round." Strive to live a holy life, and as difficult as it may be, pray for the grace of God to do so.

Making a Successful Comeback

Fall of the Man of Valor

In the Bible's entirety, David was the only man after God's heart. He was a poet, musician, courageous warrior, national statesman. There was no king in Israel like David, he was a loyal friend to the end, he possessed integrity and humility. As a shepherd boy, he defeated the bear, lion, and Goliath.

There are sixty two chapters in the Bible on the biography of David. Even through all this, David lost his battle against lust and adultery. At the age of fifty, he was unable to resist his flesh and that is where his fall began. He did not realize his wrong, and continued living life fine. Because God is a timely and precise God, he waited for

David to repent, and it took David twelve months before repenting. David did not realize his mistake until God sent Nathan to deliver the message to him

> *The Lord was with the men of Judah. They took possession of the hill country, but they were unable to drive the people from the plains, because they had chariots fitted with iron.*

(Judges 1:19, NIV)

In everyone's life, there are some mountain enemies and some valley enemies.

Characteristics of Mountain Enemies

They are giants, they are heavy, they are strong. For David, his mountain enemies were Goliath, Pharaoh, Herod, Lions, and Bears. For Moses, his mountain enemies were Pharaoh, The Red Sea, and the Amalakites. With Moses' anointing he parted the Red Sea. For Samson his mountain enemies were the lion, the Philistines and the city gate. For some people, their mountain enemies are poverty, witches, sickness, etc.

Mountain enemies make their intentions well known, but with the right anointing at the right time, they can be conquered. Some tools that can conquer them include prayer, singing, and praising, etc.

Characteristics of Valley Enemies

They have the chariot of iron, they are hidden, they are secretive. In John 10:10, their purpose is defined as stealing, killing and destroying. The valley enemies live inside a person. Every man of valor has a valley enemy. Some of these valley enemies can be adultery, anger, lust, secret affairs, cheating, stealing, etc. It takes about twenty to thirty years to build one's reputation, but it takes only a matter of seconds to lose the reputation. The most appropriate time to deal with these valley enemies is NOW; this way your destiny will not sink. Most men of valor can tackle enemies of the mountain, but it is much more difficult to tackle enemies of the valley.

David's enemy in the valley was lust, Moses' was provocation and outburst of anger, Samson's was also lust.

Before I was afflicted I went astray, but now I obey your word.

(Psalm 119:67, NIV)

Samsford says that "Trees are better measured when down." One's life cannot be truly measured until he or she is down.

Pains of Defeat

The consequences for sin are always there. One of those consequences is an absence of joy as experienced by David. Not only was he filled with sorrow, but he also lost his child, Absalom. His son rapes his half-sister and the will of God was grinding slowly until all the consequences of David's actions were manifested. God is merciful enough to forgive, but the consequences will always still come. We see that the sword never departed from David's house.

You are my portion, LORD; I have promised to obey your words.

(Psalm 119:57, NIV)

Grace is God's ability to forgive you instead of killing you straight off. Grace is God giving you the strength to endure the consequences brought on you by your wrongdoings, and it is the ability to obey God in the end. David failed, but he was able to come back. Moses likewise failed, and when he came back the consequence of his action was to see the Promised Land from afar, but not make it there. Moses prayed for others, but because he had no one to pray for him, he was not able to make it to the Promised Land.

I will instruct you and teach you in the way you should go; I will counsel you with my loving eye on you. Do not be like the horse or the mule, which have no understanding but must be controlled by bit and bridle or they will not come to you. Many are the woes of the wicked, but the Lord's unfailing love surrounds the one who trusts in him

(Psalm 32:8-10)

Making a Successful Comeback entails the following:

1. **Face what went wrong:** It is important to be honest about what happened. Write it down. 2 Samuel 12:13. Also, take responsibility for what you did wrong.

2. **Learn from what went wrong:** Figure out what you can learn from what went wrong.

3. **Cry for help:** Everyone needs God's help at a point in life. You can cry for help to God, mentors, leaders, coaches, etc. God sent Nathan in the case of David because Nathan was a man of integrity. Nathan's yes was always yes and his no, no.

Take these steps:

a) Rededicate your heart.

b) Therapy.

Disobedience to the word of God is the easiest way to fall. Let there be desperation to make resolutions. Be willing to stand by your family come what may. Watch your steps continually.

c) Return to the word of God.
Do not read the word of God for a message, but let it benefit you first.

d) Come back.

Watch and pray that you enter not into temptations.

These four words are what God is saying to you today: **I BELIEVE IN YOU.**

Prayer Points

* Father, help me to reason wisely in all situations in the name of Jesus.

* Holy Spirit, counsel me more than ever before in every step that I take in the name of Jesus.

* Almighty God, teach me purity and keep me standing in it for your glory in the name of Jesus.

* Father! I press on to maturity; take me there by your grace in the name of Jesus.

* As I press toward maturity O Lord, let every obstacle before me become plain in the name of Jesus.

Chapter Thirteen

The Characteristics of a Spiritually Mature Man
(Job 29:2-25)

෴

T he great Harry Houdini claimed he could be locked in any jail cell in the country and set himself free within minutes. And he made good on his claim in just about every city he visited, except one. That day, something went wrong. He entered the cell in his street clothes. As the heavy metal doors clanged shut behind him, he took from his belt a concealed piece of strong but flexible metal and went to work on the lock.

But soon he realized that he was not getting anywhere. For thirty minutes he worked without success. Then an hour passed. This was much longer than it usually took him, and he began to "stress out." But still, he could not pick the lock. Finally, after laboring for two hours and feeling like a total failure, he leaned against the door, and to his amazement, it swung open. It had never been locked in the first place!

How many times does something look impossible simply because you think it is? Gideon told God; "I don't have the connections" (Judges 6:15-16). Moses said, "I'm not a gifted speaker" (Exodus 4:10-17). Jeremiah proclaimed, "I'm too young" (Jeremiah 1:6-8). However, I would like to emphasize that you need to focus your faith on Him, strike the word "can't" from your vocabulary. God said in **Isaiah 41:10**: *"Don't be afraid, for I am with you. Don't be discouraged, for I am your God. I will strengthen you and help you. I will hold you up with my victorious right hand."*

And so with God's help, the impossible becomes "do-able". Today, God will make you a real man, a mature man; He will help you, *For I can do everything through Christ, who gives me strength,* as it is depicted in Philippians 4:13. (Cross references: Philippians 4:13; 2 Corinthians 12:9; Ephesians 3:16; Colossians 1:11; 1 Timothy 1:12; 2 Timothy 4:17).

Furthermore, there are some common misconceptions about Spiritual Maturity. Below are four clarifications.

Flaw 1: Because you are a Christian, all your problems are solved instantly – Have you heard "Come to Christ and all your problems will be over"? Have you ever read **John 16:33**? It says:

> *I have told you all this so that you may have peace in me. Here on earth you will have many trials and sorrows. But take heart, because I have overcome the world.*

Also **Psalm 34:19** says:

> *The righteous person faces many troubles, but the Lord comes to the rescue each time.*

In some instances, when you become more spiritually mature, problems increase, roads get tougher of course. Life is not a bed of roses all the time, but the right approach to life can help you create a full and vibrant existence

Flaw 2: All problems you will experience in this world are addressed in the Bible. Are you saying "No they're not! Most times, there is no explicit answer to a particular problem"? Work by faith and trust God to show you out of any dilemma so that you can move to the next level because without God, we can do absolutely nothing as it is portrayed in Romans 8:14: *For those who are led by the Spirit of God are the children of God.*

Flaw 3: If you are having problems, you are not spiritual. Having a problem simply means you are human. Job was spiritual, yet he had enormous problems. But the good news is that God has assured us of His presence:

> *When you go through deep waters, I will be with you. When you go through rivers of difficulty, you will not drown. When you walk through the fire of oppression, you will not be burned up; the flames will not consume you.*

> **(Isaiah 43:2)**

Flaw 4: Being exposed to sound Bible teaching automatically solves problems. No matter how gifted a teacher is the declaration of truth does not instantly remove troubles. The Bible is like a Global Positioning System (GPS) that tells you how to get to a certain destination. But you still need to drive the car, put gas in the car, pay

139

the cost, take time to travel and stay at it until you arrive at your destination. The truth is that we need to take heed to the words we hear (Psalm 119:9; 89).

By His Grace, I am blessed with three wonderful children, daily they are learning and growing. As they grow into maturity, I am delighted. So is God pleased when we grow into maturity? At first, as spiritual babies, we are fragile, irresponsible, milk-drinking infants who lack discernment and strength. But with time, we begin to grow up spiritually. Hebrews 5:11-14 emphasizes this assertion thus:

> *There is much more we would like to say about this, but it is difficult to explain, especially since you are spiritually dull and don't seem to listen. ¹²You have been believers so long now that you ought to be teaching others. Instead, you need someone to teach you again the basic things about God's word. You are like babies who need milk and cannot eat solid food. ¹³For someone who lives on milk is still an infant and doesn't know how to do what is right. ¹⁴Solid food is for those who are mature, who through training have the skill to recognize the difference between right and wrong.*

Signs of maturity could be summarized as follows:

- Practicing what you hear – it is one thing *to grow old* in the Lord (Cranky, fussy and irresponsible), but it is a different thing *to grow up* in the Lord.

- Going through a progressive process – *spiritual osmosis* – Hear, absorb, saturate yourself, act it out and live victoriously. Just like hearing the news of a growing tumor, operate on it (i.e. application).

There's no such thing as *"instant maturity"* – no formula can produce mature Christians overnight. Rather, it is a gradual process as Romans 8:19, KJV represents here that *For all creation is waiting eagerly for that future day when God will reveal who his children really are.*

Chapter Fourteen

Priorities of the Spiritually Mature Person

❧

A spiritually mature man has four priorities, which are: Spiritual, emotional, public priority and personal. Our case study here is *Job*. God says that he was "blameless, upright, God-fearing and turning away from evil.

> *There once was a man named Job who lived in the land of Uz. He was blameless — a man of complete integrity. He feared God and stayed away from evil.*
>
> **(Job 1:1)**

Spiritual Priority

Job 29:2-5 (KJV) states: *I long for the years gone by when God took care of me, ³when he lit up the way before me and I walked safely through the darkness. ⁴When I was in my prime, God's friendship was felt in my home. ⁵The Almighty was still with me, and my children were around me.*

To further buttress this point, I would like to support this quote with my own personal experience as a child growing up with my father. I remember while growing up, my daddy will place the Bible on my head on our way to church. On weekdays, if we did any wrong before my dad came back from work, the elders in the compound would whip us – heaven forbid if the matter was reported to dad; that will amount to double trouble. In those days, we respected our parents and teachers so much that we treated them like gods.

Job Had Divine Continuity with The Past

With reference to the Scriptures above, this man called Job looked over his shoulder and saw the past involvement of God in his life. He had a divine heritage. Somewhere along the way, we lost touch with that. Unfortunately today, Christian principles of living are not passed from generation to generation anymore.

The deceleration process started when fathers began sending their children to Church instead of taking them there, when they gave up on providing spiritual leadership in the home. It is sad to note that 70% of black children grow up without a father. When those children are sent off to school, 83% of their teachers will be women. If they are fortunate enough to attend Sunday school, caregivers and other leaders will be women. Women are forced to shoulder the leadership load alone and carry responsibilities God never intended them to bear.

The Divine Continuity is a Life
Totally Dependent on God

Jesus said in **John 5:19**: *"I tell you the truth, the Son can do nothing by himself."*

Remember Jesus is the only Son of God, the Word became flesh, express image of the Father, yet He said He can do nothing without God. Again in **John 5:30** He said *"I can do nothing on my own initiative,"* meaning I don't initiate a single thing. He was totally dependent on His Father.

He intones: *So Jesus explained, "I tell you the truth, the Son can do nothing by himself. He does only what he sees the Father doing. Whatever the Father does, the Son also does* **(John 5:19)**.

We must take time to pray because His instruction to us is *"We have heard it with our own ears — our ancestors have told us of all you did in their day, in days long ago:* ^{2} *You drove out the pagan nations by your power and gave all the land to our ancestors. You crushed their enemies and set our ancestors free.* ^{3} *They did not conquer the land with their swords; it was not their own strong arm that gave them victory. It was your right hand and strong arm and the blinding light from your face that helped them, for you loved them"* (Psalm 44:1-3). To be a precious vessel in the hand of the Almighty God, we need to absolutely depend on Him.

He specializes in using weak people because His strength is made perfect in their weakness. Seeking the face of God in prayer regularly is admitting your weakness to Him. For instance, Psalms 44:1-3 illustrates that:

O God, we have heard it with our own ears – our ancestors have told us of all you did in their day, in days long ago: ² You drove out the pagan nations by your power and gave all the land to our ancestors. You crushed their enemies and set our ancestors free. ³ They did not conquer the land with their swords; it was not their own strong arm that gave them victory. It was your right hand and strong arm and the blinding light from your face that helped them, for you loved them.

Job 1:5 reckons that even though Job was busy taking care of his ten children, he was not too tired to pray for them (*dependency on God*). He spent his early morning hours on his knees. He understood that a father is to be the priest of his home and maintain that continuity of commitment between generations by setting a godly example for all. It is like passing a baton to the next generation. How are you passing the baton of divine continuity?

May I ask? Are you keeping up with your walk with God? If that question does not prompt a quick yes, you are getting close to the edge! A daily walk with God is your best protection. David says in Psalm 119:11: *I have hidden your word in my heart that I might not sin against you.*

Failure is not a sin; low aim is! Living without purpose and priority is! Rejecting God is!

The other day, I saw a bumper sticker that read *"Whoever dies with the most toys wins."* You've got to be kidding! When you take your last breath, it won't matter how many toys you've acquired. You can't stop time. The question is not how long you live, but how well! The only time you have is right now! Now is the time to take responsibility for your spiritual priority – now is the time for God's favor, now *is the day of salvation* (**2 Corinthians 6:2**). *Depart from sin and sinful habits. Get out! Get out and leave your captivity, where everything you touch is unclean.* (**Isaiah 52:11**). "By Him all actions are weighed. *He will judge your actions* (**1 Samuel 2:3**)

Public Priority

The more you grow like this, the more productive and useful you will be in your knowledge of our Lord Jesus Christ.

(2 Peter 1:8)

A major sign of a spiritually mature man is his public priority. He is a man with core values coupled with character (A man of his word). Do I make decisions based on what is right or what is popular? Paul of integrity said before King Agrippa in Acts 26:19-21:

And so, King Agrippa, I obeyed that vision from heaven. [20] *I preached first to those in Damascus, then in Jerusalem and throughout all Judea, and also to the Gentiles, that all must repent of their sins and turn to God – and prove they have changed by the good things they do.* [21] *Some Jews arrested me in the Temple for preaching this, and they tried to kill me.*

Paul was very passionate about his conviction and argued successfully as the king of the land. When pretense replaces passion, we are in trouble! Do I behave differently according to who I am with?

Check Yourself In These Areas:

Can you state your core values? Before you set the goals, you must discover your God ordained purpose. Otherwise you could finish up somewhere you shouldn't be, or succeed at something God never called you to do. Or worse, your talent could carry you to heights at which your character can't sustain you. So permit me to ask about the core values of your life; are they based on what is convenient, what is cheap or what is self-serving. Refuse to live that way.

Marshall Field once offered the following twelve principles in determining your core values. We need to understand;

(1)   The Brevity of Time

(2)   The Power of Perseverance

(3)   The Rewards of Hard Work

(4)   The Importance of Simplicity

(5)   The Worth of Character

(6)   The Fruit of Kindness

(7)   The Power of Example

(8)   The Call of Duty

(9)   The Value of Economy

(10)   The Virtue of Patience

(11)   The Development of Talent

(12)   The Joy of Creativity

2 Peter 1:5-8 rightly exemplifies these principles especially that of "kindness" thus:

> *In view of all this, make every effort to respond to God's promises. Supplement your faith with a generous provision of moral excellence, and moral excellence with knowledge, ⁶and knowledge with self-control, and self-control with patient endurance, and patient endurance with godliness, ⁷and godliness with brotherly affection, and brotherly affection with love for everyone.⁸ The more you grow like this, the more productive and useful you will be in your knowledge of our Lord Jesus Christ.*

Our word is a measure of our Character: We are created in the image of God, including His moral likeness (Genesis 1:26-27). Therefore, whatever God's *Word* is to Him, our *word* is to be to us. God watches over His word to perform it. So should we. God said so and it was so. Creative power is also in man's word. In view of this, the Bible states in **Proverbs 18:21** that *"The tongue can bring death or life…"*

Therefore, words must be spoken in the fear of the Lord because we will have to account for every idle word on the Day of Judgment **(Matthew 12:36)**. Our name is only as good as our word. Satan's attack on the first family in the Garden of Eden was on "His word and His Promise to us," "Has God said…" **(Genesis 3:1)**. Satan killed the relationship when Adam denied God, and as a result, he was expelled from His presence. That will not be your portion in the name of Jesus.

Our Word is our bond: In times past, when a man gave his word and shook your hand, it was better than a signed contract; it was a covenant. Today, lawyers draw up legal contracts of an agreement. Yet, the paper is only as good as the character of the people signing it. Even in marriage, mature men vow to remain married "until death do them part." Today, in the day of drive-by wedding, such vows are no more holding grounds. For example, in Proverbs 6:1-2, the Word of God states:

> *My child, if you have put up security for a friend's debt or agreed to guarantee the debt of a stranger. ²if you have trapped yourself by your agreement and are caught by what you said.*

Our public and private word is an expression of our nature: Salvation is a total experience – inside and outside. The Holy Spirit works to cleanse us from all unrighteousness – He purges our language too. A man who uses the name of Jesus as an epithet in everyday conversation cannot be truthful on Sunday in worshiping that name. *What a shame!* To support this assertion, the book of Isaiah 6:5 illustrates this:

> *Then I said, "It's all over! I am doomed, for I am a sinful man. I have filthy lips, and I live among a people with filthy lips. Yet I have seen the King, the Lord of Heaven's Armies."*

> **(Isaiah 6:5)**

Our word is a measure of our integrity: The honesty of a man's heart and the depth of his character are revealed by how he keeps his word. It's called integrity. Job said, *"I will never concede that you are right; I will defend my integrity until I die"* (**Job 27:5b**).

God commended Job to Satan by saying, "He still maintains his integrity." Job's wife, in exasperation after all his possessions were gone, cried out against him, *"Do you still hold fast to your integrity? Curse God and die!"* (**Job 2:9**). But he would not.

Men who prove their integrity are held in admiration, great respect and are mature. Bible says a man with integrity is one who *"Those who despise flagrant sinners, and honor the faithful followers of the Lord, and keep their promises even when it hurts* (**Psalm 15:4, KJV**). In other words, he keeps his words even if it costs him his name.

Our word Earns Respect: Every week of my life, I earn the right to be respected. Next week, I must earn it all over again. If today I live on the laurels of past victories, past crown, past winning, I am living on borrowed time. Never live in the danger of living in the past. It is a daily thing – the day I say thank God, I have total victory over lust, greed, temptation, and lies. It never happens.

> *I discipline my body like an athlete, training it to do what it should. Otherwise, I fear that after preaching to others I myself might be disqualified.*
> (**1 Corinthians 9:27**)

> *So put to death the sinful, earthly things lurking within you. Have nothing to do with sexual immorality, impurity, lust, and evil desires. Don't be greedy, for a greedy person is an idolater, worshiping the things of this world.*

(Colossians 3:5)

Job's Testimony

> *Those were the days when I went to the city gate and took my place among the honored leaders.[8] The young stepped aside when they saw me, and even the aged rose in respect at my coming.[9] The princes stood in silence and put their hands over their mouths.[10] The highest officials of the city stood quietly, holding their tongues in respect.*

(Job 29:7-10)

Earning respect is very different from simply expecting respect. A mature man behaves in such a way that you have no choice but respect him. Job went to the gate of the city (That's downtown) and sat in the square (City council/City Hall). The young men saw him and said, "We've got to go, Mr. Job is here!" They didn't say, "Ain't nobody gonna tell me what to do!"

While growing up, when someone older than you comes around, you get up – law of kindness and respect was operating. They are looked upon as helpless, easy prey victims. A person who does not respect his father, how can he respect strangers?

The older men and his elders rose up when Job came to the scene – Job commanded respect. The princes (yuppies – smooth talkers, business men) stopped talking when Mr. Job walked in. He changed the environment, set the standard. Why would people respect you when every word from your mouth is profanity, and in perverted language?

Emotional Priority

We do this by keeping our eyes on Jesus, the champion who initiates and perfects our faith Because of the joy awaiting him, he endured the cross, disregarding its shame. Now he is seated in the place of honor beside God's throne. ³Think of all the hostility he endured from sinful people then you won't become weary and give up. ⁴After all, you have not yet given your lives in your struggle against sin.

(Hebrews 12:2-4, KJV)

Whatever Jesus did, He did it with His whole heart, enthusiastically, full of energy and Passion! Passion!! Passion!!! (**Passion** – is the fire, the desire, the strength of conviction and the drive, the locomotion which sustains the discipline to achieve the vision. Let people see the fire in your bones. Preaching must be emphatic; else, it won't affect others.

If you can't do it passionately with all your energy, vigor and with deep sense of passion, then step aside. Do you know why Satan tried so hard to destroy you? He knows if you ever line up your passion with God's purpose for you, there will be no limit to how far you can go - *Al-*

leluia! Passion is a spiritual energy; without it, you are as limb as wet spaghetti and as bland as hospital food. God wants you to be either hot or cold. Cold if you are saved, but hot if you have surrendered your life to Him because He wants us to be good stewards of His grace in our lives. In other words, God does not tolerate us being lukewarm as portrayed in Revelation 3:15-16:

> *I know all the things you do, that you are neither hot nor cold. I wish that you were one or the other! 16 But since you are like lukewarm water,* **neither hot nor cold, I will spit you out of my mouth!**

"Never hot or cold, I wish you are one or the other." Ask God to rekindle the flames of passion in your soul and *"get going"* for Him.

Child-Raising Commitment

> *The Almighty was still with me, and my children were around me.*
>
> **(Job. 29:5)**

"My children were around me" – he wasn't showing up at the tent after the kids went to sleep, or rushing them to bed just to get them out of his hair. He was surrounded by these ten kids – much more is caught than taught.

Contrary to today's belief that family planning is far better than having many children, the Bible states in Psalm 127:5, NIV that *"blessed is the man that has his quiver full of them..."* Today, many people believe that, children are a drain on our energy and resources. How about my retirement, Cadillac, Armani suits – this is the pagan way of thinking.

The Man is Stable

In Job 29:18-19, the Word of God states *I thought, "Surely I will die surrounded by my family after a long, good life.¹⁹ For I am like a tree whose roots reach the water, whose branches are refreshed with the dew."*

To lay more emphasis on the above quote, here is a clearer illustration: A man who knows what God has called him to do, will depend on Him to do it through him. Families today do not formidable foundation because they lack purpose and direction. Many move *helter skelter*, looking for the good life, but ended up being disappointed because their lives are out of order. Their plans for the future are self-centered whims. A mature man may be on the move like Abraham, but his family knows where he is going, and they can draw strength from his dependability.

A Man of Justice

Also in Job 29:14-16, the Bible states thus:

> *Everything I did was honest. Righteousness covered me like a robe, and I wore justice like a turban.¹⁵ I served as eyes for the blind and feet for the lame¹⁶ I was a father to the poor and assisted strangers who needed help.*

A mature man does not justify wrong in any way because he knows that wrong is wrong any day. He is not a politician watching for the crowd reaction and applause.

He is not intimidated by race or riches – refuses to trade truth for popularity. Our children are joining gangs and cults - alternative families where they think they can find love, attention, self-esteem they didn't experience at home – *because dad wasn't around.*

His Attitude Speaks Volumes

An Olympic gold medalist once said "I believe the only difference between gold and silver medal winners is their attitude, not their ability."

> *Guard your heart above all else, for it determines the course of your life.*
>
> **(Proverbs 4:23)**

You need to develop a winning attitude and become a coach of the same. By now, it is very obvious that attitude is the route to the heights.

Personal Priority

Have you stood in front of a full mirror lately? Pay close attention to yourself. Are you eating properly? Are you resting properly? Are you eating too much and becoming fat? Are you holding a grudge? Are you out of balance? *Pay attention to yourself?* Somebody once said that self begins from looks. Looks are a function of personality.

David is a great example for this illustration:

> *Then Samuel asked, "Are these all the sons you have?"*

*"There is still the youngest," Jesse replied. "But he's out
in the fields watching the sheep and goats." "Send for him
at once," Samuel said. "We will not sit down to eat until
he arrives."¹² So Jesse sent for him. He was dark and
handsome, with beautiful eyes. And the Lord said, "This
is the one; anoint him." ¹³ So as David stood there among
his brothers, Samuel took the flask of olive oil he had
brought and anointed David with the oil. And the Spirit
of the Lord came powerfully upon David from that day
on. Then Samuel returned to Ramah.*

(1 Samuel 16:11-13)

God wants you to know that if you don't take a break, you
won't get one. He wants you to survive the long haul not
just the short sprint. The first enemy you need to send
home is loneliness and guilt. That's what makes us all
"workaholics". We feel guilty resting because there's just
"so much to be done." But Jesus felt differently, "come ye
yourselves apart…and rest."

*Then Jesus said, "Let's go off by ourselves to a quiet
place and rest awhile." So they left by boat for a quiet
place, where they could be alone.*

(Mark 6:31-32)

Some do not set aside time to eat? No time to take care
of themselves? "I was told, it's better to burn out than to
rust out" – that's a poor advice. You can't burn out doing
the will of God, Jesus said, *"My yoke is easy, and my burden
is light* **(Mark 11:30)**. Why? The crowd did not set His
agenda – *His father did* **(John 5:19-20)**. David said, *"He
maketh me to lie down…"* He leads me beside peaceful streams
(Psalm 23:2). Wouldn't you rather go to the park by choice

157

than to the hospital by force? No, God won't send you there, but your lack of wisdom will.

Read **Mark 6:3**:

> *Then they scoffed, "He's just a carpenter, the son of Mary and the brother of James, Joseph, Judas, and Simon. And his sisters live right here among us." They were deeply offended and refused to believe in him.*

Therefore, appreciate your life as you look at the mirror.

A Mature Man Has Wisdom

> *Everyone listened to my advice. They were silent as they waited for me to speak. And after I spoke, they had nothing to add for my counsel satisfied them.²³They longed for me to speak as people long for rain. They drank my words like a refreshing spring rain. ²⁴When they were discouraged, I smiled at them. My look of approval was precious to them. ²⁵Like a chief, I told them what to do. I lived like a king among his troops and comforted those who mourned.*
>
> **(Job 29:21-25)**

You do not need a college education to be wise. The world is full of well-educated fools. Real wisdom is the ability to take God's truth and apply it to life. All it requires is a heart for God and some plain old common sense. Whatever your level of wisdom, you can always ask God for more just as the Bible made it clear in James 1:5 that *If you need wisdom, ask our generous God, and he will give it to you. He will not rebuke you for asking.*

What to do and How to do them:

(1) Let your schedule reflect your commitment.

(2) Be a churchman – be accountable to other men like you who want to be God's kind of man.

(3) Develop the God kind of love – be committed to Love in actions, not feelings.

Any dog can satisfy his libido. It takes a truly mature man to be faithful regardless of his passions. He sacrifices anything that interferes with his calling as a husband, father and churchman. That you have failed in the past does not make you a failure. Get back on your feet, confess your sins to God, recommit yourself to spiritual priorities, dust yourself off, and *"go and sin no more."* Praise the Lord!

PRAYER POINTS

- Father! Endow me with character commensurate to maturity in the name of Jesus.

- Holy Spirit, help me to live a life of maturity in Jesus' name.

- Holy Spirit, I don't care what it costs me; keep me under your control.

- From now on, O Lord, let my priorities be divinely set in the name of Jesus.

- From now on, O Lord, let the words that I speak first pass through your mouth in the name of Jesus.

- Almighty God, break me and take me to the Potter's house for a remolding in the name of Jesus.

- I have no power of my own, Holy Spirit, I look up to you, help me in the work that I have been called to do in the name of Jesus.

Chapter Fifteen

Living to Impact Your Generation

∽

A life is not significant except it has an impact on other lives. God created man to make impact from generation to generation. God gave to mankind different levels of knowledge, gifts and skills so that we can relate with one another. Each individual has his own unique abilities and personality that the others who don't have it will need. Therefore, everyone has what it takes to make an impact. You are expected to affect and influence others positively. Right from the beginning of creation God made this provision.

> '*And God blessed them, and God said unto them, Be fruitful, and multiply, and replenish the earth, and subdue it: and have dominion over the fish of the sea, and over the fowl of the air, and over every living thing that moveth upon the earth'.*
>
> **(Genesis 1:28)**

The relevance of a man is in the impact he makes; otherwise he is a waste of space and a disappointment to his generation and to God. Although we are all equipped with what it takes to make an impact, only a few make impact in every generation. What does it take to impact your generation? We shall examine this by looking at the exploits and impactful life of Philip in three outlines:

Outline 1 - From Ordinary to extraordinary
Outline 2 - The Pressure that brings out the best
Outline 3 - A life of Impact

Outline 1 – From Ordinary to Extraordinary

Philip was one of seven deacons consecrated in **Acts Chapter 6** to serve tables. Serving tables sounds so ordinary that no one could have imagined an extraordinary impact down the line. How could a "table server" or an Usher have made such a great impact that brought a major revival to a city? .

> *[7]For unclean spirits, crying with loud voice, came out of many that were possessed with them: and many taken with palsies, and that were lame, were healed. [8]And there was great joy in that city.*
>
> **(Acts 8:7-8)**

It is in the nature of God to move people from ordinary to extraordinary. Out of the seven deacons, only two of them impacted their generation: **Stephen and Philip.** The others have no second mention in the Bible beyond the day of their ordination.

You can make impact where you are and with what you have; no matter how ordinary it looks or sounds, because what you have is needed to impact your generation. All that you need to make impact is already in you.

David was a shepherd boy and he was very ordinary. His brothers despised him at the battlefield. Even the King told him how ordinary he was to think of fighting Goliath.

And Saul said to David, thou art not able to go against this Philistine to fight with him: for thou art but a youth, and he a man of war from his youth.

(1 Samuel 17:33)

How can ordinary people do extraordinary exploits and impact their generation? There are 6 key points with the acronym *"impact"*.

I - **Identify your Talent and Assignment**
M - **Make the best use of every opportunity**
P - **Pray without Ceasing**
A - **Adventure and Accountability**
C - **Christ-centered**
T - **Teachable**

1. Identify your Talent and Assignment

It is important to identify your area of strength. The talent is there, the assignment is waiting but it's for you to discover. Moses undoubtedly had a seed of greatness in him, but did not identify it on time. At eighty, he was still an employee of his father-in-law, when he was supposed to be a commander-in-chief of the great army.

How Moses kept the flock of Jethro his father-in-law, the priest of Midian: and he led the flock to the backside of the desert, and came to the mountain of God, even to Horeb.

(Exodus 3:1)

163

At eighty, God had to intervene in the life of Moses as he was wasting away. He has spent two-thirds of his life and he was yet to discover his assignment. Until you discover your assignment you are far from greatness. Even when God intervened in the life of Moses to help him discover his seed, he almost lost it.

> *"And Moses said unto God, Who am I, that I should go unto Pharaoh, and that I should bring forth the children of Israel out of Egypt?"*
> **(Exodus 3:11)**

David identified his talent on time, as a teenager, he killed lions and bears. When it was time to battle with Goliath, he knew there was an assignment for him and nothing could stop him from going for it. He declared to the whole nation in the battle field his readiness for this assignment (1 Samuel 17:33-37).

Stephen saw more than serving the table. For him it was a total package and he went for it. God will intervene in your life and lead you to your divine assignment.

There is a story that has been told about a King who had only one daughter. He gathered all the Young Men in His domain around a crocodile infested river. He sought to know who is the most courageous and who among them can he commit his Kingdom to his hand. Who will passionately take care of my only daughter? He thought. He felt the test should be the ultimate test. Whoever can swim across the crocodile infested river and come out alive will get to rule the Kingdom and marry the King's

164

only daughter. All the young men gathered around the river and no one dared swim the waters because everyone saw the impossibility of the mandate. The people discussed, and spoke about the challenge and the impossibility and the fact of the distance and the obvious tails of the hungry crocodile ready to snap a bone.

All of a sudden, there was a big splash! Someone was in the water! Everyone could see the crocodile circling and a young man began to swim the swim of his lifetime! He swam so strong and so powerfully that before you could blink your eyes really, he was on the other side of the river. There was a loud shout, the land has found its champions, every other young men looked at this swimmer in awe. He made it! He will rule the Kingdom, he will get to marry the Kings daughter. While everyone was busily congratulating the young man, he asked for silence. He looked over the audience and quietly asked them: "May I ask, which one of you pushed me into that water?" WHO PUSHED ME?

Sometimes, we need someone to PUSH US for us to get to the optimum status that God desires for our lives. Will you allow yourself to be pushed?

2.   **Make the best use of every opportunity**

Daily life is your fundamental context for making an impact on others, be it in your home or at work. The next sphere is your church where each believer should be serving selflessly. Biblically the church is not an event we attend, it is a family to which we belong and in which we participate. The church is not somewhere we go. It is something that we are. You are the Church.

The Bible says,

> *Each one should use whatever gift he has received to serve others, faithfully administering God's grace in its various forms.*

(1 Peter 4:10)

The point is that God's Spirit is working in each one of us uniquely, as he entrusts us with gifts and holds us responsible for the way we use the gifts. God is the source, supply, and supreme end of our service. We serve with God's gifts using God's words and God's power for God's glory. Through and through our service is God-centered.

Philip made use of the opportunity to serve tables and because he was faithful in ordinary things he got assigned an extraordinary task.

> *He that is faithful in that which is least is faithful also in much: and he that is unjust in the least is unjust also in much. ¹¹If therefore ye have not been faithful in the unrighteous mammon, who will commit to your trust the true riches?*

(Luke 16:10-11)

3.   Pray without Ceasing

Prayers work wonders! No wonder the Bible tells us in *1 Thessalonians 5:17, "Pray without ceasing".* There was need for Joshua to command the sun to stand still in one direction and the moon in the other. He did not waste time, he prayed.

> *"Then spake Joshua to the LORD in the day when the LORD delivered up the Amorites before the children of Israel, and he said in the sight of Israel, Sun, stand thou still upon Gibeon; and thou, Moon, in the valley of Ajalon."*
>
> **Joshua 10:12**

God is waiting for the Joshua of our time who will pray to make impact. Philip prayers made a difference and yours can make a difference too (James 5:16 - the effectual fervent prayer of a righteous man avails much).

4.   Adventure and Accountability

Adventure - Life is either a daring adventure or nothing. The difference between ordinary and extraordinary is simply that little word "extra". Change will not come if we wait for some other person or some other time. Adventure is the game of winners and men of impact. The Adventure of Philip in Samaria brought about a City revival.

> *⁵Then Philip went down to the city of Samaria, and preached Christ unto them.*
>
> **(Acts 8:5)**

It is never too late to be who you are made to be – Begin the Adventure now!

Accountability - Being accountable is being answerable. Be careful of those who want responsibility without accountability. Responsibility minus accountability is a disaster! You must have someone you answer to. For "power corrupts, absolute power corrupts absolutely!"

'so then we must all give account of ourselves to God".
(Romans 14:12)

You're not accountable until it costs you something to pay for what you have done! A saying by Admiral Rickover goes thus: *"Unless you can point to a specific person to hold responsible for an action, then you had no one truly responsible.*

* Studies done in factories have proven that both quality and quantity of workmanship increases when employees know they are being observed. If only we can realize His eyes are on us, our behavior and attitude to sin will change.

* Personal accountability is invaluable. I was encouraged to hear about the practice of the men who followed John Wesley in his lifetime. They meet once a week as small groups and they are committed to one another's purity. They pray with and for one another. They talk openly and honestly about their struggles, weaknesses, temptations, and trials. In addition to these general things, they look one another in the eyes as they ask and answer no less than **seven specific questions:**

1. Have you been with a woman this week in such a way that was inappropriate or could have looked to others that you were using poor judgment?

2. Have you been completely above reproach in all your financial dealings this week (pay all your bills, etc.)?

3. Have you exposed yourself to any explicit material this week?

4. Have you spent time daily in prayer and in Scriptures this week?

5. Have you fulfilled the mandate of your calling this week?

6. Have you taken time off to be with your family this week?

7. Have you lied or have you sincerely answered the previous questions?

5.   Christ-centered

Philip was Christ-centered. His message was about Christ, His love, redemptive power, salvation, healing, and deliverance. We are to be Jesus's hands and feet, showing and sharing His love. The Spirit of God empowers us to serve with the abilities he gives us. We are responsible to be good stewards of the abilities God has entrusted to us to serve others. We have just one message and it is *Jesus Only*. He is the Savior, sanctifier, healer, and baptizer and…there is no other name apart from His name (Acts 4:12)

Jesus tells us that each one of us matters. We each have a part to play. You are needed. Church is not a spectator sport. Every Christ-follower is on the playing field. Can you imagine in the middle of a soccer game, one player refused to play, grabbed a chair and just sat down on the edge of the field? Every Christ-follower should have a regular life rhythm of impacting others because the Father commands it, Jesus models it, and the Spirit empowers it.

6. Teachable

Keep trying and stay humble. The proud is too arrogant to learn but the humble is teachable.

> *"Likewise, you who are younger, be subject to the elders. Clothe yourselves, all of you, with humility toward one another, for "God opposes the proud but gives grace to the humble."*
>
> **(1 Peter 5:5)**

You are unlikely to find a man of impact who is not teachable. Having a teachable spirit is something that most people lack and that's why the list of people of impact is a shortlist. People that are not teachable have the following traits:

- They never feel secure about their identity, and are constantly comparing themselves to others.
- When someone corrects them, they get defensive.
- They won't take advice from people not like themselves.
- They are the kind of people who are constantly trying to prove something.
- They may tend to lie to make themselves look good in front of others.
- They are ashamed to let others know who they really are.

- When they are corrected, they typically feel rejected.

"Whoever loves discipline loves knowledge, but he who hates reproof is stupid."

(Proverbs 12:1)

These vital points translate ordinary people to extraordinary ones. You are made for impact. There are however levels of impact and the level of impact has a lot to do with the challenges on the way and that takes us to second outline

Outline 2: The Pressure that Brings out the Best

There was a sequence of trials, challenges and persecutions that preceded the exploit of Philip in Samaria. His friend and co-laborer; Stephen was stoned to death. Now the attack was intensified and death beckoned.

And Saul was consenting unto his death. And at that time there was a great persecution against the church which was at Jerusalem; and they were all scattered abroad throughout the regions of Judea and Samaria, except the apostles.

(Acts 8:1)

The pressures, trials and persecutions led Philip to Samaria. The problems, trials and persecution you are going through may be all you need to bring the best out of you.

The persecution and hatred of Joseph was needed to fulfill his destiny. The conspiracy against Daniel that landed him in the Lions' den took him to heights he never dreamt of. David needed Goliath for his prominence.

Are you facing trials and temptation? That may be what you need to make the right impact.

- When Trials and Temptations come TRUST GOD (Job 13:15)

- When Trials and Temptations comes PRAY MORE (Luke 18:1)

- When Trials and Temptations come STEP UP (to more service) — From serving Tables to preaching Christ.

> *⁵Then Philip went down to the city of Samaria, and preached Christ unto them.*
>
> **(Acts 8:5)**

A life of impact is God's plan for us and that takes us to the final outline.

Outline 3: A life of Impact

> *¹²Verily, verily, I say unto you, He that believeth on me, the works that I do shall he do also; and greater works than these shall he do; because I go unto my Father.*
>
> **(John 14:12)**

God's desire is that we do exploit much more than He did while on earth.

Philip continued to make impact after the exploit in Samaria.

Then the Spirit said unto Philip, Go near, and join thyself to this chariot.

(Acts 8:29)

The Ethiopian eunuch received Salvation and was baptized by Philip. To live a life of impact you must be filled with the Spirit of God.

Then the Spirit said to Philip, "Go near and overtake this chariot."

(Acts 8:29)

The power of the Holy Spirit is crucial for a life of Impact. Even the Lord Jesus Christ had to rely on the anointing of the Holy Spirit in His earthly ministry (**Acts 10:38**). However the Holy Spirit comes only on Holy vessels. The Passion for holiness passes on the power of the Holy Spirit.

⁹Thou hast loved righteousness, and hated iniquity; therefore God, even thy God, hath anointed thee with the oil of gladness above thy fellows.

(Hebrews 1:9)

Each of us should be engaged in purposeful living. This is living to represent Jesus, living on purpose. Realize that you are already deployed into a mission field. You are a sent one! Jesus said,

"As the Father has sent me, I am sending you."
(John 20:21)

The word for "sent" is related to the word "missionary."
Every Christ follower is a missionary right where you
live. Christ followers reproduce regularly. We reproduce
disciples of Jesus. We are called to multiply. So we impact
others by living purposefully in our daily lives.

Love must be the motivating force in all that you do,
especially for others in Christ. You have the River of
love flowing in you by the Spirit of Christ that is in you.
Love is your nature in Christ. Let that love dwell within
you and constantly motivate you to godly acts that will
impact <u>others</u>. Make it a point of duty to impact as many
people as possible in your life time. Live your life in such
a way that you will be remembered for the good that you
have done like Philip.

⁸And there was great joy in that city.
(Acts 8:8)

The Significant Impact One Person Can Have

In an overpopulated world, it's easy to underestimate
the significance of one person. There is a tendency to
think and to feel that m*ost people are more capable and more
important than I am. Who am I, anyway to think that I could
make a difference? I must ask you, is this how you feel?*

History is full of single individuals who have made a
difference. You must be glad that Henry Ford, Martin

Luther King Jr., Winston Churchill, Abraham Lincoln, Deborah and Paul believed that One Person indeed can make a difference. Think about the following:

- How many did it take to rescue the man on the Jericho Road? Just one good Samaritan.

- How many did it take to confront Pharaoh and lead the Exodus? One man – Moses.

- In 1645, one vote gave Oliver Cromwell control of England.

- In 1649, one vote caused Charles I of England to be executed.

- In 1776, one vote gave America the English language instead of German.

- In 1845, one vote brought Texas into the union.

- In 1868, one vote saved President Andrew Jackson from impeachment.

- In 1923, one vote gave Adolph Hitler control of the Nazi party.

- In 1941, one vote saved the selective Service System just 12 weeks before Pearl Harbor!

You can make an impact too. Please read the following Scriptures:

2 Chronicles 16:9; Isaiah 59:15-16; Jeremiah 5:1; Ezekiel 22:30.

Chapter Sixteen

Making an Impact
(Judges 9:8-15)

⬿

A parable is meant to illustrate a deep truth, which simple minds might not fully understand. When a thought needs to be clarified, the wise use parables to bring understanding and decipher meanings. One thought that requires such clarification is this: how does a person make a wise decision in the midst of multiple captivating offers? A wise person should note that certain offers and promotions (that many other people long for) should be turned down. The above parable in Judges, spells out what it means to make an impact and make decisions in the midst of captivating offers.

Child of God, God has a glorious destiny for you and He is ready to perform His word. However, your commitment, the strength of your decision, the power of your will shall be tested. Your consecration and your dedication will be proven—they have to be genuine otherwise, the enemy will derail you. Usually, God will not approve a life He has not tested.

In the parable of the trees in Judges 9:8-15, a decision had to be made by trees in the forest. The olive tree, fig tree and the vine were asked to be king over trees. Unfortunately, these trees declined the offer, but when the trees approached the thorn bush and offered the same opportunity to him, they got an affirmative response. Unlike the previous trees, the thorn bush accepted willingly. Irony is applied here: valuable plants did not accept a good offer; a useless plant accepted the splendid position.

The conspiracy: The enemies conspired against Mr. Olive. They did not do this through a noticeable sin but by a type of temptation that any human being would easily yield to: PROMOTION! It was a very cheap and attractive offer - no cost, no strings attached. Certain categories of Christian workers/ministers are targeted in the realm of the spirit because of their commitment to divine service. Ordinarily, if the situation were normal, the trees would not go past tall, upright, and robust trees to the olive tree and the fig tree and ask them to become the king. No! Whenever people offer a minister something that is too cheap, something that is too good to be true; such a minister should have a discerning mind and 'smell a rat'. Often, in such situations, there is a hidden agenda. Your prayer should be: Every conspiracy against my destiny, Father, frustrate them in the name of Jesus!

Six things you need to do to make an impact:

1. Know & Abide in your Calling (vs. 8-9):

God's calling and His purpose for the olive tree is primarily to generate oil. Its gifting is from above and it produces without stress. It does not do this for personal glory but for the prosperity and lifting of men and for the glory of the Almighty. Without him, no king or priest can reign in his domain. Can you imagine testimonies, countless thanksgiving and anointing services occasioned by the faithful service rendered by Mr. Olive. Everybody is praising God for Mr. Olive.

Characteristics of the Trees:

*   Olive: Most plentiful in Palestine (called land of olive oil - Deuteronomy 8:8-10); their roots don't die (can live for 1000 years), leaf is evergreen. It is picked when green; when ripe, it is full of oil. Ripe olives are shaken, beaten from the branches and pressed. A tree can yield 10-15 gallons of oil. The oil is used for cooking and as butter. People burn olive oil for light and for warmth; it is used to eliminate friction on machinery. God appointed Olive Oil for the anointing of Kings and Priests and for other sacred uses (Exodus 27:20, Exodus 30:22-30, Leviticus 12:10-12, I Samuel 16:13, Psalm 133:1, Matthew 24:1-12).

*   The Vine: This plant cannot stand-alone. It has to attach itself to a tree or to other support to get off the ground into the air and into sunshine so that it can bear fruit. Its fruit are in clusters. It is full of juice that are easily pressed out for wine (Psalm 127:1-3, Isaiah 5:1-7, Matthew 21:31-45). The Vine makes glad the heart of men and of King, and it makes faces to shine. Wine from the Vine is used on wounds (Luke 10:34).

- Fig Tree: It bears fruit without visible flowers. It has large leaves and is dark green. It is an irregular tree. It bears fruit before the leaves appear. Fig tree fruit is sweet and nourishing, possessing soothing and healing powers (2 Kings 20:7, Isaiah 38:21).

- Thorn Bush: This shrub is not a picture of what is heavenly. It is rather a picture of what is selfish and cruel. When the attempt to entice the olive tree failed, the antagonists shifted their focus to the fig tree. In the same manner, the fig tree queried the hidden agenda and said,

> *Should I cease my sweetness and my good fruit, and go to sway over trees?*
>
> **(Judges 9:11)**

The same thing happened to the Vine, the sweet 'counselor', the one who cheers God and man. They all rejected this evil offer because *they highly esteemed their present invaluable contribution to the deliverance and the functioning of mankind.* They treasured their eternal reward as having a far greater value than the promised temporary worldly satisfaction.

Olive, fig and vine trees are very valuable for the need of mankind. They were dignified enough and secure enough not to consider the position of a king as being more important than their primary call. They see such a *promotion* as useless and a waste of energy. On the other hand, the thorn bush, an insignificant plant saw it otherwise, he wanted to be king.

Remember this statement very well: **A <u>Career</u> is something you choose, a <u>Calling</u> is something you receive.**

A career is something you do for yourself; a calling is something you do for God. A career promises status, money or power. A calling generally promises difficulty, suffering and the opportunity to be used of God. A career may ends with retirement. A calling is not over until the day you die. A career can be disrupted by any number of events, but when God calls you He enables you to fulfill your calling even in the most difficult circumstances.

Know your calling and abide in your calling. Pray, "Father lead me not into temptation of abandoning my calling..." A calling abandoned is a Life destroyed!

2. Your Decisions Determine your Destiny:

The parable spells out what it means to make decisions in the midst of captivating offers (Deuteronomy 30:19, Joshua 24:14-21). The Olive, Fig and the Vine knew their calling; however, they had to make decision to abide in it.

The loneliest place in leadership is reserved for the person who makes the first decision. The leader who will not make decisions creates insecurity among followers and a platform for potential leaders who recognize a decision must be made. A CEO of a major corporation once said: "95% of the decisions you make as a leader can be made by a reasonably intelligent teenager. They simply require common sense. However, you get paid for the other 5%"

- The wrong decision at the wrong time = DISASTER
- The wrong decision at the right time = MISTAKE
- The right decision at the wrong time = UNACCEPTANCE
- The right decision at the right time = SUCCESS

Wisdom cries out in the street, but few listen (Proverbs 1:20). God's wisdom almost always surfaces when we simply pose the question: What is the wise choice? Always ask the question: Who will benefit the most from this decision? You or others? God or others?

3. **Desire to be the Best:**

Make an impact and have a hunger for excellence. John Maxwell, one of the nation's top authorities on leadership, says this concerning excellence:

Excellence is:
- Paying attention to every detail,
- Always striving to do better,
- Giving 110% effort,
- Going the extra mile,
- Doing the job right, even if it means working longer hours.

Psychology Professor Jon Johnston points out the difference between **"mere success"** and **"excellence"**. He said, *"Success bases our worth on a comparison with others; excellence measures us against our own potential. Success grants its rewards to the few but is the dream of the multitudes. Excellence is available to all living beings, but it is accepted only by the few."*

Paul in Philippians 3:14 says, *"I press toward the goal for the prize of the upward call of God".*

My prayer for you is that you will not die unsung, un-heralded and ordinary.

4. Work on your Attitude:

Your attitude determines your altitude. You are the product of what you imagine, think, feel and act upon (Proverbs 23:7; Genesis 11:6). Your attitude will either make you or break you.

Have a positive image of yourself and believe what the scripture says about you (1 Peter 2:9; Philippians 4:13). Rediscover yourself. Who are you? What is your purpose? Where are you currently in relation to where you should be? (Genesis 3:8-9; 1 Chronicles 4:9-10).

Ignite with passion the giant in you to perform within God's niche, to assume its rightful position with development and progress as his ultimate goal (2 Corinthians 4:6-7). Stagnation brings extinction. Position yourself to your individual assignments and pursue set goals to the end (Hebrews 12:1-2).

Be daring not only to go for Gold but Diamond as well. We must climb the mountain and reach the pinnacle of anything we set our minds to (Joshua 14:7-12). Show your faith.

5. Be Disciplined:

Ripe olives are shaken, beaten from the branches and pressed for oil to come. To be disciplined sometimes means doing what you do not want to do or not doing something you want to do. The world lies at the feet of disciplined people. The race is not won by the talented, intelligent, gifted or well-connected people (Ecclesiastes 9:11); they are won by the disciplined. Medals never rest on the chest of the undisciplined.

One sorry moment of unrestrained lust rained disaster not only on Amnon himself but also on all those around him (2 Samuel 13). He could have inherited the throne of his father.

Like auction, we need to set boundaries before we meet the situation that tests them. Before the offer for kingship was made Olive, Fig & Vine had defined their boundaries. Have you?

6.   **Prayer is the Key:**

*"Howbeit this kind goeth not out but by **prayer and fasting"***

(Matthew 17:21)

We find that we need to go down on our knees and seek the face of God in fervent prayer until the anointing comes and the glory falls, then we impact the world for Christ. James 5:16 says, *"The effectual fervent prayer of a righteous man availeth much."* There is no short cut. It takes fasting and prayer. God wants to break the yokes. He wants to bring deliverance. His desire is for us to be saved, healed, and blessed, in order for us to walk in the anointing on a daily basis. We must have a continuous attitude of prayer so the power of God can flow through us.

I believe we can preach holiness and live a life of separation and still see the miraculous and the supernatural demonstrated. No prayer, no revival! **John Knox** is a great example of someone who prayed and experienced great revival in his time.

The anointing will change the natural, normal, ordinary Church into a supernatural power house of signs, wonders and miracles. The anointing of the Holy Ghost comes through fervent prayer. To secure the anointing in our churches, and do exploits, we must pray.

THE COMMISSIONING

The Olive tree (Oil); Fig tree (Fruit); and the Vine trees (Wine) all have to die to allow the next generation to take over. This singular act will determine their destiny and position their posterity for greater impact.

The highest form of recognition that a teacher can give a follower is "go and teach in my name." Fulfilling commission is the highest complement and act of gratitude the student can give the teacher.

When Jesus first called the disciples from their careers as fishermen, they brought their life experiences and skills to the new task. Within the three years of staying under the leadership of Jesus, they were Transformed, Equipped, Inspired and Spiritually grounded to become leaders who fulfilled the great commission:

- Starting out, He told them, *"Follow me and I will make you..."* (Matthew 4:19).

185

- At his departure, He told them, *"Go ye therefore and make disciples of all Nations, teaching them to observe all things I have taught you, lo I am with you always"* (Matthew 28:19-20)

They went through four stages of learning:
- **Novice** – These are beginning leaders, they are just starting out. In Matthew 4:18-20, they were enthusiastic; however, they had no clue on how to complete the task.
- **Apprentice** – These are leaders In Training. In Matthew 17:15-16, a father with a son who had seizure and the disciples couldn't heal him. In verses 18-20, Jesus healed the boy; however, he told them why they couldn't do it, *"...ye have little faith"*
- **Journeymen** – Somehow capable of working on their own. They still need to be told where and when to apply their skill. An example is Peter walking on water – Matthew 14:26-30.
- **Master/Teacher** – Now they are highly skilled and able to teach others. Hear the message of Peter in Acts 2:36-41, under the anointing 3000 were saved and baptized. Fully developed skills with confidence, motivation to produce excellent result.

What are you doing to pass along that which has been given to you to next generation?

It is a privilege to:
a. Develop people who not only are able to do the task on their own but can also teach others (2 Timothy 2:2, Matthew 28:19-20).

b. Send someone out to act on your behalf. It is the highest form of validation of your trust in that person's competence and commitment (Matthew 28:19-20).

The church has the promised potential of plenty of power and God's glory (Deuteronomy 8:7-10). It seems we are being attacked on all sides, but let us keep our focus on Jesus Christ. Keep moving forward.

Prayers:

- Let's pray that all our entangled soldiers, our derailed and distracted 'Moses' and 'Demas' would hear the alarm and the battle cry and return to base, not fearing the wrath of their Pharaohs.

- If you're not yet a victim of this temptation, you need to pray for grace that never takes the adversary for granted. Paul said, 'we should not be ignorant of his (Satan's) devises. The antidote to distraction is Discipline!

Chapter Seventeen

Maximizing Your Leadership Potential
(1 Chronicles 11:15-19)

‿

As a student, there was a type of test I dreaded. They were not multiple choice questions because one can usually guess the right answers. Essay questions are not as hard either, just come up and drape your uncertainty in complex phrases and convoluted sentences. Use enough words and you might confuse the teacher. However, the most difficult ones are the fill-in-the-blanks because you either know it or not. In life, you cannot afford to be ignorant concerning some vital questions. You cannot make an impact without maximizing your leadership potential. Three words need defining: *Maximizing, Leadership* and *Potential.*

Maximizing: Making as great as possible, increasingly becoming greater or larger; to assign the highest possible importance to your assignment.

Leadership: It has been described as a process of social influence in which one person can enlist the aid and support of others in the accomplishment of a common task. There are as many definitions of leadership as there are many leaders.

My definition is simple: *Leading people without manipulation.* Jesus led a bunch of cynics, people with anger management issues, rogue tax collectors, thieves and rough untrustworthy fishermen to be world changers!

Potential: Possibility or capable of becoming possible, as opposed to actual. For example, potential energy is inherent energy. It is energy unexpressed. Potential energy is not fully appreciated in its idle state. On the other hand, kinetic energy is expressed in a moving object.

Every object possesses energy, though in different magnitudes. You cannot fully appreciate the power possessed by an object that is static. You cannot also appreciate the power a coconut fruit hanging on the tree has until it falls on your head. Whenever an object moves, there is an additional force that acts on the potential energy, making it more useful and effective. It is called kinetic energy or the moving force. The impact of a gasoline tanker parked in a lot cannot be compared to its impact when it is moving. To make impact in your world, your potential need to be put into action.

Examine the story of David and some of the men that joined him at the Cave of Adullam (1 Chronicles 11:15-19). They were miserable men, full of potentials and when David was promoted king, they became David's mighty men.

The question is: What set these men apart? How did they maximize their potentials?

There are some things that are quite unique about these 400 men (1 Samuel 22:1-2). What they did can be seen in 2 Kings 19:30, *"And the remnant who have escaped of the house of Judah shall again take root downward, and bear fruit upward."*

A. They expanded their horizons (trading known for unknown)
B. They were willing to break new grounds
C. They maximized their "today"

A.   They expanded their horizons:

We live under the same sky, but we do not all have the same horizon. Expanding your horizon means being able to see greater potential that is all around you; it means to increase your range of view. Whenever your horizons get widened, the way you view life changes. Things around you are perceived differently. If what you did yesterday still looks big to you, it means you have not done much today. Whoever is afraid of doing too much always does too little.

Incorporating new ideas, treading on an unfamiliar terrain, increasing the number of your customers, learning new things, going from local to global in your area of influence among several others are synonymous to widening one's horizons. For instance, having realized the need for global relevance, part of the steps taken by **James Dyson** (a manufacturer of vacuum cleaners) to widen his scope of influence, was continuous innovation of new range of *Dyson Ball* machines and opening of branches of the company in new territories.

Amazingly, the company now sells vacuum cleaners in 45 countries worldwide.

The impact and spread of the Gospel was small after the Pentecost due to the fact that the disciples were still myopic and ignorant of the great commission handed down to them in **Acts 1:8.** Today, it has spread across the world when they decided to see beyond their noses.

Do not be afraid to take a big step if it is required. You cannot cross a chasm in two small jumps. Learn new things, make new friends and visit new places. Keep imagining expansion, see beyond where you are. Attempt something new and something bigger than you.

Look around, then look a little farther, then look a little farther still. What can you see? Do you see your service or products being enjoyed globally? This will naturally plant the seed of expansion or provoke a sense of growth.

The force of stagnation is broken in your life. The door of new innovations is now opened for you. See you on top!

Prophetic Prayers

- Let the spell of smallness be broken by your anointing upon me.
- Silence the fear that has been preventing me from taking giant strides (2 Timothy 1:7).
- I am not a local champion; I refuse to operate below God's expectation.

B.   They were willing to break new grounds

Geography makes a difference sometimes. Some crops do well in certain locations but not so well in some other locations. For instance, pineapples do well in Hawaii, but they do not do very well in Alaska. Atmosphere really matters and climate is important for any seed to grow. In the same manner, you are a seed. Your products and services are like seeds. A business is like a seed; hence, you may need to change locations and situations to unlock the full potential of your success.

Breaking new grounds means walking on unfamiliar terrain, operating under a different climate, networking with new people, changing locations or trying something new. Success requires people. You may never experience success without networking with many different kinds of people. They may not be easily accessible. You may have to leave the comforts of your home or office to reach them.

Jesus was constantly in motion, changing locations. He was constantly arising, departing and going to new places as can be seen in the following Bible references:

> *[1]When He had come down from the mountain, great multitudes followed Him. [5]Now when Jesus had entered Capernaum, a centurion came to Him, pleading with Him. [14]Now when Jesus had come into Peter's house, He saw his wife's mother lying sick with a fever. [23]Now when He got into a boat, His disciples followed Him. [28]When He had come to the other side, to the country of*

> *the Gergesenes, there met Him two demon-possessed men,*
> *coming out of the tombs, exceedingly fierce, so that no one*
> *could pass that way.*
>
> **(Matthew 8:1, 5, 14, 23, 28)**

Abraham, the patriarch of the Israelites, had to make geographical changes before his success was birthed (Genesis 12:1-2). Joseph found his incredible breakthrough in another country (Egypt). Ruth willingly left her heathen family in Moab and went with Naomi to Bethlehem, where she met and married Boaz, a financial giant of the community. Andrew Carnegie's life was never meaningful in his native land – Scotland, until he migrated to the United States.

Yours may not necessarily require a change of location; it could be a change of company or adoption of a new strategy. Nonetheless, some people and opportunities will not come to where you are. You have to go to them. Sometimes, you may have to go somewhere you have never been before in order to taste the extraordinary success that you desire. So, be prepared to move. From today, your life will assume a new coloration. You will be relevant to your generation. See you on top.

Prophetic Prayers

- Dear heavenly Father, thank you for the good plans you have for me.
- Grant me the willingness to go to where I have never been before.

3. They maximized their "today"

"Whatever your hand finds to do, do it with all your might, for in the grave, where you are going, there is neither working nor planning nor knowledge nor wisdom."

(Ecclesiastes 9:10)

Maximizing today is sowing the seed for a better tomorrow. The seed of tomorrow you are clamoring for and eagerly expecting is in today that you have. Yesterday has gone, why cry over a spilled milk? There is nothing anyone can possibly do about it. You do not have any control over tomorrow either. But what you and I have is today, whatever you do today will determine how tomorrow will be. Someone said 'Each day that passes without a recordable achievement is a waste'. Life is not a dress rehearsal. I do not care what philosophy you believe in, we have only one shot at this game called life.

The stakes are too high to waste your life. The question is; what time is it and where are we? The answer is now and we are here. The message is not that you do not need to plan for the future. The message is you need to plan for the future. The fact is that if your today is productively maximized, you have sown the seeds for a better future. No wonder Ecclesiastes 9:10 clearly illuminate our minds that our best time is now, not tomorrow. Some people practice procrastination by hiding behind high-sounding words, saying 'I'm analyzing' and six months later they are still analyzing. What they do not realize is that they are suffering from a disease called: **Paralysis by Analysis.**

Some procrastinate by saying, **'I am getting ready'**. A month later they are still getting ready and six months later they are still getting ready.

Take note, the saddest words in life are: 'It might have been', 'I should have', 'I could have', 'I wish I had'. If you want to build a positive attitude, learn the phrase, 'Do it now'. Make the best out of now and utilize the present to the fullest.

Remember, time flies. Years roll by unnoticed. Before you realize what is going on, they would have gone by before your very eyes. See every second of your life as something you must account for. Secure a focus on time. Spend all your energy to pursue it. Avoid all time-wasters. God will see you through. Receive grace now to be diligent.

Prophetic Prayers

- Holy Spirit, engage me in a productive venture, I disconnect from all   time-wasters in Jesus' name.
- I receive divine wisdom to manage today, grant me the correct perspective of life.

COMMITMENT TO INVEST

"Do your best to present yourself to God as one approved,
a workman who does not need to be ashamed and who
correctly handles the word of truth."
(2 Timothy 2:15)

There are countless opportunities for investment
in ourselves. Investment is not restricted to money. Everything you say or do creates an investment somewhere.
But whether that investment generates a dividend or
loss depends on you. It is a great mistake to believe
that you are working for someone else. No matter how
many bosses you may have, God is the real and ultimate
employer. Investing in yourself makes you better, more
skillful, more marketable, more relevant, more competent
and more enjoyable in whatever service you are rendering.
Fulfillment of destiny is impossible without you applying
the principle of investing in yourself.

Making time to take your spouse and children out for re-
laxation, refreshment and other forms of recreation is a
good investment for marriage. Reading at least one or two
pages of vital information relevant to your assignment on
a daily basis is also a good form of investment. Giving to
people, organizations or the needy is worthy investments
into your future because it will always come back to you in
multiples (Luke 6:38).

Spending quality time and money to acquire training,
attend seminars, conferences and workshops will make
you a better person. Participating or engaging in regular

physical exercise from time to time and eating nourishing food is an enormous investment into your health.

Watch out for opportunities to invest, and put in your best. What you plant now will be harvested later. Gilbert Arland said it correctly: **'To improve your aim, improve yourself '**. When prosperity comes, do not consume it all. Give some back to others and invest some in yourself.

Time spent in investing or improving yourself is never a waste. God's presence will surround you. His favor will envelope you.

Prophetic Prayers

- Open my eyes to investment opportunities around me.
- I receive abundant grace from above to maximize opportunities sent to me for investment.
- I bind spirits behind laziness and misplacement of priority; they cease to operate in my life.

GAINING MASTERY

"After Jesus had gone indoors, his disciples asked him privately, "why couldn't we drive it out?"
(Mark 9:28)

When a violinist plays a perfect piece of classical music in a concert, or when a singer sings professionally well in an exquisite opera, no one ascribes their accomplishment to luck. When a craftsman builds a beautiful piece of furniture, elegant and refined in every detail, no one explains or dismisses such achievement as having been a matter of good luck. As a matter of fact, in every case, when you see someone do something in an excellent fashion, you recognize and appreciate a work of mastery.

Several weeks, months and even years of hard work and detailed preparation normally precede an excellent performance of any kind. As His response to the question put to Him by His bewildered disciples upon their failure to drive out demons from a possessed person, Jesus said; *"No one gains mastery over demons except he/she is spiritually empowered"* (Mark 9:30, Paraphrased). Several days of fasting, prayers and meditation that Jesus had subjected Himself to gave Him such unusual and unquestionable authority.

Nido Qubein, a highly rated and legendary speaker in America, when asked about the secret of his outstanding performance on stage said, he would often invest as many as 100 hours of planning, preparation and rehearsal for a one-hour talk that he would only give once to a single audience. There is no short-cut to mastery in any field. Any man who can patiently go through the rigor of training and ultimately come up with a means of doing or producing anything better, faster or more economically, will always have his future and his fortune at his fingertips.

The level you are is not God's intention for you. There's still room for improvement. Take your time, and spend your money to access the fundamentals or principles of your profession. Go for more training. Rehearse constantly in your closet if need be. Look for those who are authorities in your field and get close to them. Read their books; learn their secrets, *because there is a secret to every mastery.* Except you are the best, you will always be among the rest.

Go and shine. You are a star!

Prophetic Prayers

- My seat among mediocre is destroyed. I receive power from on high to maximize my destiny in Jesus' name.

- I connect to the grace to be a high flyer in my field and area of calling in Jesus' name (Esther 2:15,17).

- Amazing power of creativity and supernatural achievement become my portion from today in Jesus' name.

- Oh Lord, take me beyond the limit of my imagination.

WORKS CITED/REFERENCES

Ben Stein: Entrepreneur Quotes

Blackaby, Henry and Richard Blackaby (2011) "Spiritual Leadership: Moving People to God's Agenda", *B & H Publishing Group Nashville, Tennessee*, P.149.

David Kavenhill, (2007). "Surviving the Anointing; Learning to Effectively Experience and Walk in God's Power", *Destiny Image Publisher Inc,* Shippensburg PA.

Ellis Cory, (2009). "Growing Up Without Father: The Effects on African American Boys". University of Wisconsin.

Merriam-Webster's Dictionary (2001) 10th edition. http://www.merriam-webster.com/dictionary/responsibility

Ogden, Greg and Daniel Meyer, (2007). "Leadership Essentials: Shaping Vision, Multiplying Influence, Defining Character". *InterVarsity Press IL,* P.153.

United States of America Congressional Record: Proceeding Debates of the 106th *Second Session, Volume 146, Part 15.* Washington D.C.. UNT Digital Library http://digital.library.unt.edu/ark:/67531/metadc31033/. Accessed July 29, 2012.

BOOK REVIEW

~

This book serves three major purposes for a reader regardless of your purpose of reading. The depth of knowledge is an excellent resource for any research minded individual; the insight provided gives direction to the curious and the theme provides inspiration to those who aspire to be great. The bonus is that it is written with such a great craft and with such simplicity that it gives one the ultimate reading pleasure. It is indeed a pleasure reviewing this book.

Every page reveals thoroughly researched, well-articulated Biblical truths presented in a simple easy to read language. The book opened with the requirements of a leader, goes on to compare a shepherd with a hireling. The author outlines the responsibilities of a spiritual leader while also engaging the mind of his readers with God's plans, provision and expectation not just for His chosen leaders but also for every serious minded follower of Christ. Three chapters are dedicated to how as a leader or an aspiring leader one can maximize one's leadership potential by living to make an impact.

Leading leaders, aspiring leaders, trainers of leaders alike, will find the contents of this book very useful. Practical in its presentation, visibly enthused with the passion of its author, 'RIGHT LEADERSHIP - Making Impact Today' is a book that will go down in history as timely and much needed in the body of Christ at such a time.

The author's writing style is reminiscent of Jesus' teaching style of presenting divine truths through parables. I love how the story of farmyard animals giving report of their day's activities and basking with pride, remind us of how ministry is all about God and not us!

Aptly captured as "The Seven Deadly Siphons", the author in a subtle yet profound manner directed readers' attention to what I term 'Leadership Madness' in the body of Christ - " leaders who are pursuing personal agenda at the expense of Kingdom agenda, holding onto position, building empires as if they are already in their destination." He reminded such leaders that "time spent in a position is a privilege and opportunity for training and exposure."

Pastor, Dr. Fadel equally admonished spiritual leaders to avoid the same mistakes made by fallen leaders and to put safeguards in place by being aware that "you are not indispensable..." He wrote further, " It is striking to observe how oblivious many leaders are to the dangers within. We do not even recognize the envy, laziness, pride and self-conceit, intellectual pride, misplaced affections within us." He counseled wrongdoers to engage in self-examination and give up areas of disobedience, lest your growth be truncated and you end up in frustration! The book not only dwelt on the spiritual wellbeing of leaders but also their emotional wellbeing and physical appearance!

On a final note, I wish to congratulate our Dr. Fadel on blazing the trail for many Pastors and leaders by putting together this wonderful resource on leadership, re-echoing the Biblical phrase in the Book of Revelation that states: "Let him that has ears hear what the Spirit is saying."

I look forward to a revised edition, which hopefully will touch on the heart cry of the younger generation for exemplary leadership among the older generation.

Having read this book, I highly recommend all leaders, aspiring leaders, and trainers of leaders to read the book and imbibe its principles. Thankfully, we can attest to the fact that the author has not only put theory across to us but ideals, which we see him, practice.

Pastor Sir, congratulations again, may more books come forth from the fountain of wisdom where this came from.

Pastor Bimpe Ishola

ABOUT JAMES FADEL

Born on April 5th, 1958 into a devout Catholic family, Pastor Fadel, as he is fondly called, tells of how he carried his father's Bible on his head as they went to church every Sunday. After he graduated with honors in junior college education in Nigeria, he relocated to the United States in 1982 on a Nigerian - Western State study scholarship. Pastor Fadel received a bachelor's degree in Mechanical Engineering and Applied Mathematics from the Western Michigan University in 1986 and also achieved a successful professional career with the Ford Motor Company as a Mechanical Engineer.

Rising to the position of Senior Design Engineer with key achievements in lead positions, he later obtained a Master of Science degree in Operations Research from Wayne State University in 1990 followed by an M.B.A. degree from the Lawrence Technological University, Michigan in 1993. He continued with subsequent entrepreneurial achievements in metropolitan Detroit. In 2012, he completed his Doctorate degree and earned a Doctor of Ministry (D. Min) from Bakke Graduate University.

Having committed his life to the Lord in 1973, Pastor Fadel joined The Redeemed Christian Church of God (RCCG) in Nigeria in 1975 and continued to serve the Lord in the US with a passion that culminated in a call to ministry. He also attended the Bible College of Birmingham in order to prepare himself for what he knew was God's purpose for his life.

Mentored by the General Overseer of RCCG, Pastor E. A. Adeboye, Pastor Fadel pioneered a home fellowship in his basement in 1991. By 1992 this developed into the first parish of RCCG in North America – Winner's Chapel, Detroit. In 2001, Pastor Fadel was appointed the Chairman, Board of Coordinators of RCCGNA.

Under his leadership, RCCGNA has grown to over 700 parishes in 64 zones. Each year thousands attend the annual RCCGNA convention at the over 700-acre campground in Floyd, Texas. Pastor Fadel also works tirelessly to develop other national programs to enable RCCGNA ministers and workers to develop and mature in their Christian walk and service.

By the grace of God, he is happily married to Pastor Manita, a medical doctor specializing in the area of pediatric medicine, and they are blessed with three children.

To order more copies of this book,
contact us using the information below:

Fadel Publishing International

515 Country Road 1118
Greenville, TX 75401
www.jamesofadel.com
info@jamesofadel.com